GAIA'S KITCHEN

GAIA'S KITCHEN

Vegetarian Recipes for Family & Community

Julia Ponsonby
and friends at Schumacher College

CHELSEA GREEN PUBLISHING COMPANY
White River Junction, Vermont

First published in 2001
by Chelsea Green Publishing Company
P.O. Box 428
White River Junction, VT 05001
800-639-4099
www.chelseagreen.com

in association with
Schumacher College
The Old Postern, Dartington
Totnes, Devon TQ9 6EA
www.gn.apc.org/schumachercollege

Schumacher College is a department of
The Dartington Hall Trust, a charity registered
in England, no. 279756

Typeset at Green Books, Totnes, Devon, UK

Designed & produced by Rick Lawrence +44 1803 865931

Photographs © Kate Mount 2001
Photographs © Nick Philbedge 2001

Vegetable & fruit drawings by Antonia Spowers
Owl cartoons by Kath Dalmeny
Diagrams by Julia Ponsonby

Printed by Kingfisher Print & Design Ltd, Totnes, Devon, UK

Library of Congress Cataloging-in-Publication Data
available on request

ISBN 1-890132-89-6

CONTENTS

ACKNOWLEDGEMENTS

Thanks must go first and foremost to Helen Chaloner, who began the recipe book project, and who taught me to tear lettuce—carefully. Secondly I would like to thank Alice Pitty, Schumacher's second 'kitchen fairy', who continued to work with the recipes and brought tempeh and breadmaking to the College. I would like to thank John Lane for encouraging Helen to embark on the project in the first place, and for continuing to encourage me; Lis Himmeroder for spurring me on to revive the project once it had fallen into an abyss, by offering to type up recipes; and Olga Kropikova, who went on tapping my recipes into the computer when Lis had left; Anne Phillips for cheerfully giving her invaluable time and energy to carry out editorial work on the manuscript, sorting out finances and all the nitty-gritty details of production; William Thomas for all his technical assistance and ideas; Jane MacNamee for her invaluable address list, reading, commentary and support; Janice Young for her marvellous help with emails and other computerized details; Gideon Kossoff for helping with the booklist and perfecting the quantities of spices in certain recipes; John Elford for his skilful brewing up of green tea and this Green Book.

I would also like to thank Kath Dalmeny for her bright enthusiasm for the project and her brilliant owl cartoons; Antonia Spowers, a sculptress, who agreed to make drawing vegetables part of her work when she came here as a volunteer-helper, and was so generous, gracious and modest about it; and Sophie Reynolds for being my special diets consultant. Inge Page and Hilary Nicholson have also been enormously helpful, acting as consultants for various recipes—and I would like to thank them for reading the manuscript and putting up with all my questions. At a more analytical level, conversations with Helena Norberg-Hodge on the economics of food production have been very insightful, as have the visits of Vandana Shiva to Schumacher College; Jenny Pidgeon, Director of Dartington's Regional Centre for Organic Horticulture, gave up her busy time to explain developments at the market garden; whilst Mary and Lucy Bartlett filled me in with many fascinating details about its history. Thanks also to the Bartletts for rescuing us at a critical moment with their freezer; to Steve Course and all at the Dartington Pottery for allowing us to use their beautiful vessels in our food photographs; and to the Cider Press Centre for lending some elegant props.

Next I would like to thank all those cooks who have contributed recipes and ideas to the cookbook, and all the people who have loved and looked after the College kitchen. Amongst them have been the participants and teachers who have provided the unceasing momentum for this project by suggesting (several times on each course), "Why don't you make a recipe book! It would be a sell out!"—they too deserve many thanks for their constant prodding (and we hope they are happy with the result!). Lastly, but not least, I would like to thank my partner Stephan Harding, my mother Ursula, and Satish Kumar, all of whom have encouraged me to continue writing—as well as cooking—and who have never ceased to support this particular recipe-writing venture with a keen eye on its completion.

Dartington Hall

SETTING THE SCENE

Schumacher College
Dartington's Harvest
The Zen of Cooking
Cyclical Activity

The Old Postern (home of Schumacher College)

SCHUMACHER COLLEGE

Schumacher College was founded in 1991 upon the convictions that the world-view which has dominated Western civilization has serious limitations, and that a new vision is needed for human society and its relationship to the Earth. It seeks to promote the human-scale values in which E.F. Schumacher, author of *Small is Beautiful*, so passionately believed.

Evidence of planetary crisis confronts us, both in the form of ecological degradation and through the loss of meaning experienced in our lives. Increasing numbers of people are seeking to understand the complexities of this breakdown, and are wondering whether and how to invest their own lives in making a difference. The College offers rigorous inquiry to uncover the roots and ramifications of a world-view that is destabilizing natural systems and traditional ways of living. It explores alternative approaches that embody holistic rather than reductionist perspectives, and ecological rather than consumerist values. These approaches are diverse, and today permeate the domains of economics, psychology, science, business, religion, ecology and art.

Through its work, Schumacher College aims to explore and to help form the foundations of a new world-view. Key thinkers, writers and activists from all around the world engage with an equally international group of students to explore the critical issues of our time. Intellectual inquiry is only one part of a unified education that embraces physical work, field trips, meditation and creativity in a mosaic of learning that reflects the wholeness of life. People find refreshment, and often new direction. They find that they have touched a source of inspiration and are reminded that there are others who share their deepest values about life and its meaning.

Schumacher College offers residential short courses ranging from one to three weeks in length as well as a one year masters programme in Holistic Science. For all students the gracious, time-honoured Old Postern building becomes a home from home. It is a place not only for reflection and stimulation, but somewhere that frequently becomes a base for exploration of Dartington and the surrounding countryside of South Devon. The College is set on the Dartington Hall Estate, which has been a focus of radical experimentation in education, the arts and commerce over the last 75 years. Beyond lies Dartmoor with its rock tors and semi-wild ponies; the rugged coastline with its beaches and coastal paths; and the beautiful small town of Totnes with its markets, health shops and lively alternative scene.

At a practical level, everyone who comes to study at Schumacher College engages in the day-to-day process of sustaining the college. This includes cooking, as well as cleaning and occasional gardening. People find that working together in small groups is an enjoyable experience, and helps to generate a sense of community. Through preparing a delicious vegetarian diet together, participants discover new possibilities for living more lightly on the planet, where an over-emphasis on meat production and fishing has become a source of ecological imbalance.

DARTINGTON'S HARVEST

People often ask whether we grow our own vegetables at Schumacher College. The answer is always a rather hesitant "No, but . . ." We have little more than a few herbs, some edible flowers and some rhubarb growing in the college kitchen garden. But Schumacher College is just one department within the Dartington Hall Trust, which is based on an 800 acre estate, where one of the other activities is a market garden. And if you asked whether the Trust grows its own vegetables, the answer would be: yes, more and more.

Just 200 yards up the road from the college, the Dartington organic market garden is to be found nestling on the hillside below the spectacular formal gardens that surround the medieval hall at the centre of the Estate.

The market garden provides the College with many of its vegetables. In July the garden and polytunnels are abundant with potatoes, lettuces, tomatoes, cucumbers, basil, peppers and aubergines. Come January, winter salad and leeks are still available. What the market garden cannot provide we buy in from Riverford Farm—a much larger organic farm two miles down the road. We are very lucky to be situated in Devon, where the scale of organic production is expanding, and it is inspiring to see the Dartington market garden (now re-named the Regional Centre for Organic Horticulture) becoming more and more a central player in this movement at an educational level.

The recent history of horticultural education at Dartington dates back to the 1950s, when a training programme for master gardeners was begun. This course soon became renowned for turning out some of the highest calibre gardeners in the land. If you had acquired a Dartington Hall diploma in horticulture it was considered you were likely to be a true craftsman in the art of gardening—flowers, hedges, vegetables, fruit, glass houses, garden design, the lot. Dorothy Elmhirst (who bought the Estate with her husband Leonard in 1925) was herself a very keen gardener. The director of the horticulture training programme in the 1960s and '70s, Terry Underhill, always looked upon her as his major inspiration in matters of garden design. He keenly looked forward to regular meetings with her, where, over tea and chocolate cake, they would discuss their beloved garden.

In 1993, under the direction of Marina O'Connell Brown, the market garden began its conversion to organic production—ahead of the rest of the Estate's land. The market garden began to produce fruit and vegetables for the White Hart restaurant at Dartington Hall, and for Schumacher College. The layout of the market garden follows not only organic but permaculture principles. Thus the original concept was to involve animals as well—and a huge dray horse was brought in to give a first initial ploughing to part of the land. After that, much mulching began!

These developments in organic horticulture need to be seen in the context of the changes on the Estate and in the surrounding county of Devon. Indeed, the swing towards organic production at Dartington is part of a much larger awakening to the value of 'real food' throughout the Western world. At a national and local level this has lead to attempts to evolve an infrastructure that supports local organic growing. For example, since 1998 over ten farmers' markets have been started in Devon, enabling small-scale growers to find local outlets for their produce.

On the rest of the Dartington Hall Estate's farm land, the process of conversion to organic is now well underway. In a sense, these ecological changes at Dartington can be seen as a living demonstration that Schumacher College is doing

SPECIAL DIETS

People's dietary needs are, of course, only 'special' relative to social context. Indeed, many people in Britain still regard vegetarianism as a strange and unhealthy diet, fit only for rabbits!

For people unfamiliar with vegetarianism there is still some confusion about what most vegetarians will eat; and a failure to distinguish lacto-vegetarianism from veganism. Some hosts may assume that a vegetarian guest will eat fish, whilst others assume that he or she won't eat cheese. In fact, no true vegetarian will eat any flesh, whether feathered, furry, scaly or slimy—nor will they eat anything that implicates the death of animals. For example gelatin allows cows' hooves to loiter invisibly in the sweetest and fluffiest of desserts and jellies! But unless vegetarians actually say they are vegan, they will, in theory, eat cheese, milk, butter and eggs.

There are many people who choose to cut out red meat (and perhaps chicken), whilst continuing to eat fish—but it would be a mistake to call these people vegetarians. They are really reformed carnivores, trying to do what they can to regain balance in a society that sometimes seems to have gone burger-mad. Likewise, no true vegan will eat eggs—but some people use the term loosely as a shorthand for conveying the fact that they are avoiding all milk products due to a lactose intolerance. In contrast to this, a Brahmin may wish to avoid eggs for religious reasons, but be quite happy with milk products.

As the variety of foods available has increased, so too has the variety of special dietary needs. Not only do more ingredients travel greater distances ('food miles') to ever more places, but more happens to these foods before and after they arrive at their destination. Some people think it is the hybridization and processing of ingredients that cause many allergic reactions—not to mention the use of pesticides. However, many Eastern systems of medicine, as well as homeopathy, associate certain foods with certain health conditions and physiological needs. Other people will also say that in the natural state of affairs, the variety we are now confronted with would not be available. Our bodies would therefore naturally adapt to a simpler regional diet that echoes what the land underfoot can grow (which may, of course, include meat). This links us with our place, and gives us an appropriate diet for it. Complementing this thinking, we have seen the rise of a movement promoting organic and local food take off in recent years, seeking to undermine the globalization of our diet, for reasons of health, ecology and economics.

But for some people an intolerance to lactose, gluten or nuts is not what causes them to adopt a special diet. They may feel a passionate identification with our fellow creatures and their treatment—or they may be following a spiritual path that prohibits the consumption of animal products and certain other ingredients. For example, we have occasionally had participants who want to avoid onions and garlic for religious reasons. Both in Hinduism and Sufism eating onions and garlic is considered to be passion-forming and not recommended for people practising meditation.

Today, many people go to alternative medical practitioners for help with their health, and this frequently results in dietary observations. Both Chinese medicine and homeopathy frequently recommend deleting certain ingredients from your diet as part of a health cure. Conventional medicine also recognizes the importance of diet. The standard diet recommended by doctors to reduce the risk of cancer is typically one that is low in animal fat, fried food and salt— and high in raw vegetables and fruit.

Whatever the reasons for deciding to try out a special diet, you should, of course, maximize its chances of working. This means making it as easy as possible to adapt to the changes, so that you don't pine for the diet you are used to. Are there any general guidelines that can help? When discussing this with Sophie Reynolds, a long-term volunteer who has attended many courses and helped with facilitation, she emphasized the following:

"I have had to follow a vegan and wheat-free diet for several years now, mainly for health reasons. The most important thing I've realized is not to be shy about it! Own your diet! If you're going to a dinner party or out to lunch with friends tell your host/ess your requirements in advance. This gives them the opportunity to make something special for you—for you to explain why you'll only be eating the vegetables, or to offer to bring something extra along for yourself. Otherwise your poor hostess will be left wondering what's wrong with her cooking, or having to scrabble around for something different for you at the last minute. I have found people only too willing to support my diet once they understand what it's about—often in a very creative way!"

The next thing is to chat to someone who has been using a similar diet to you, to find out the tricks they have developed; or to read up about it. If you've decided to be a vegan, then a vegan cookbook may help you to maintain variety in your diet (see Booklist). It will also help you evolve a diet that allows you to combine the foods you can eat so that you realize their potential and escape from merely trying to imitate 'normal' diets.

Specialist cookbooks aside, the key thing when adapting recipes for a special diet is becoming skilful in the art of substitution. From the point of view of a host or hostess catering for a special diet, they should not panic and feel they have to make one guest a completely different meal, but realize they will most likely have many suitable ingredients in the menu they have been planning already. Creating an appropriate special diet will often be no more than a matter of deleting a few elements and cooking the remaining ones separately.

Here are a few ideas to guide you in the art of substitution.

Butter substitution

In baking, use margarine instead of butter, but check the ingredients list on the label carefully: many margarines contain milk products such as lactic acid, lactose and skimmed milk. Kosher margarine will always be reliably dairy-free. Sunflower, corn and soya oil can also be used as a butter substitute, but use about a quarter less by volume, since both butter and margarine contain wet, non-fat elements such as water or whey, which oil does not.

Egg substitution

In sweet recipes, try substituting each egg with half a mashed banana (approx. 2 oz) or with 2 tbsp vinegar. Recipes with lots of eggs, such as meringues, macaroons or sponge cake, are better avoided. If the dough holds together without a substitute, you may not need to use one—as in many cookie recipes. However, if the dough seems crumbly, try adding soya milk, soya dessert, or linseeds ground and blended with soya milk. To glaze bread, biscuits and pastries, paint on soya dessert. This has a custard-like consistency and will glue down nuts and seeds, giving a 'satin' finish when baked.

In savoury recipes, try replacing each egg with 1 tsp soya flour blended with 1 tbsp water, or 60 g (4 tbsp/2 fl oz) smooth peanut butter or tahini, or 60 g plain tofu blended with 1 tsp water; 60 g (4 tbsp) mashed potatoes can also be used. Use whichever substitute seems appropriate. Very small quantities of eggs (e.g. in some pastry doughs) can simply be left out, and a little more water or soya milk added to assist binding. Again, you should not expect substitutes to work in recipes where there are lots of eggs. However, recipes for vegan mayonnaise and vegan 'cream' are given on pages 138 and 187. In these, almonds and soya milk substitute for eggs to produce a surprisingly light, almost gelatinous sauce. Successful quiches can also be made by blending tofu (see under cheese substitution).

Wheat substitution

People often follow a wheat-free diet because they have an allergy to gluten (or to find out if they do!). Gluten is the elastic element in bread that expands like bubblegum when the yeast grows, allowing bubbles to form, which makes for a light, airy loaf. It is present in a greater volume in wheat than in any other grain—but it is nonetheless present in other grains, such as oats, rye and barley. People with an extreme allergy to gluten may have to avoid these flours as well, and confine themselves to breads made with buckwheat, soya, maize, gram (lentil) and rice flour. Special gluten-free bread and flour mixtures can now be bought in health shops. Gluten-free bread often tastes better when toasted.

It is helpful to distinguish between two medical conditions in which wheat frequently becomes a problem. With coeliac disease, the gluten in wheat, rye and oats causes the allergic reaction, whereas with *candida albicans* the reaction is not only to gluten but to yeast, sugar and any other fermentation-promoting ingredients, such as mushrooms, vinegar and fruit.

In both cases it will be necessary to avoid use of wheat, and if breads or sauces are to be made, to use gluten-free flours instead (and omit yeast in the case of the candida sufferer). For a coeliac, all products need to be scrutinized to check they contain no wheat, rye, oats or barley. This will obviously mean no pasta, no breadcrumbs, no biscuit and no semolina.

A gluten-free loaf of bread will be much more crumbly than normal bread, and heavier. Sometimes I find it helps to make the dough moister (like thick porridge) and add a few eggs to help bind the ingredients together. You can use yeast in the case of the coeliac diet, but not when making bread for someone with candida. In this case, use baking powder instead.

When making a white sauce, use cornflour or arrowroot to make the roux. Since these are purer starches than wheat flour, try using half the volume. You can add a little extra cornflour or arrowroot later, if the sauce is still too thin once boiling point has been reached—but be sure to blend it in a little cold water first, or you may get lumps.

Wheat-avoidance definitely seems to be on the increase, and is also prescribed by many Chinese medical practitioners. It is interesting to note, however, that spelt flour—made from an ancient strain of wheat—does not appear to provoke the same allergic reactions. However it is better to consult your doctor before using it as a substitute for normal wheat flour. Spelt makes very good brown bread—similar to a standard wholewheat bread, and not too heavy.

Milk substitution

A large percentage of the world's population simply does not possess the enzyme necessary to digest cow's milk. When Nestlés attempted to undermine breast-feeding in the developing countries by selling dried milk powder to mothers, the scandal was made worse by the fact that many babies could not even digest it. However, certain enzymatic changes that occur when yoghurt is made mean that many people who find milk a problem can consume yoghurt. Similarly, goat and sheep milk may not be a problem—but cannot, of course, be used as a substitute in vegan diets where all animal products are avoided on principle. Soya milk, rice milk and water can be used as a substitute for cows milk etc.. Technically speaking, both these products are in fact classified as 'drinks' by the food authorities. But colloquially speaking, 'milk' seems a suitable term for any edible white liquid (be it from coconut or cow), so I shall continue to use it here. Since rice milk is slightly sweet, it should not be used to make savoury sauces, but is good on cereals and in cakes. If sheep's milk is to be used in sauces, it can be diluted half and half with water. Many people also like to use fruit juice instead of milk on their breakfast cereals.

When adding soya milk to soups, boil it separately first and add it just before serving. Be sure not to boil soup with soya milk in it, as it coagulates far more easily than cow's milk. Similarly, if you try adding a dash of soya milk to strong coffee it will curdle—and you would be better off boiling some up and making a milky 'cappuccino style' brew (it froths up well). With tea, there appears to be no such problem.

A form of soya yoghurt can be made out of soya milk, and this can also be purchased quite easily nowadays—as can soya cream. When making your own soya yoghurt, the easiest thing is to use normal live yoghurt as a starter—if this is acceptable.

When using soya milk to make a white sauce, don't worry if the sauce doesn't appear to get as thick as with milk. It will thicken up later on when the dish you are creating gets baked (i.e. in a vegan lasagne).

Always buy organic soya milk, as soya beans have been one of the first casualties of genetic engineering. But as previously mentioned, no products (to date) labelled 'organic' can contain genetically modified ingredients. Sometimes you will need to check the small print to see whether minor non-organic ingredients are included—and if these non-organic ingredients include soya lecithin, it is worth checking with the store keeper that the manufacturers guarantee their product is from a GMO-free source. Fortunately, this usually appears to be the case with products described as organic.

A final tip is that if soya milk or soya yoghurt tastes 'beany' you can try adding a tiny drop of vanilla essence. Just a little will usually remove the beany flavour without introducing a vanilla one.

Sugar substitution

People requiring little or no sugar in their diets will often be suffering from candida or diabetes. They may also be on a slimming diet, or trying to be healthier. With respect to the candida diet, all sweet products will be out of bounds including fruit, dried fruit and honey, so there is no point in looking for natural substitutes. Since this diet also requires avoidance of wheat and butter, attempts at cookie and cake making will be difficult! Other savoury treats will just have to be found. Sweets using artificial sweeteners may not be as sweet as they seem at face value—especially if they contain aspartame, which has been shown to be carcinogenic.

Moving to the area of diabetes, it is the day-to-day diet that really counts, and the occasional treat does no harm. Normally, people suffering from diabetes will take charge of their own diet and not expect a host or hostess to do it for them. They may need to know what time they will be eating so they can coordinate their insulin injections with this. They may also be involved in carefully measuring their carbohydrate intake; having a ready source of carbohydrate (pasta, bread, rice, potato) at each meal can be a help.

Lastly, more and more people seem to prefer to eat a low sugar diet for health reasons, or simply to opt for only using natural sugars, avoiding highly refined white sugars. Most recipes can have sugar levels reduced and brown sugars used instead of white sugar. Dried fruits such as dates and figs also act as a good natural sweeteners, and can be chopped finely and used instead of all or some of the sugar. Soaking these fruits in boiling water for several minutes, or overnight in cold water, can make them easier to chop (or mush) up. Honey is another excellent natural sweetener that can be used in teas and fruit salads, and you can use it as a substitute for sugar in cake baking. Though you may lose some of honey's nutritional benefits through cooking with it, the main consideration is perhaps whether you like the rather interesting taste cooked honey produces. Also, if honey is runny, you may need to cut down the other liquids in your recipe in order to obtain the desired consistency. Malt extract and rice syrup may also be used in this way.

As far as a slimming diet is concerned, using substitute natural sugars will not necessarily reduce calorific intake. Sugar is a bit like salt, in that the more you eat it the more you crave it. Gradually re-educating your palate by eating less sugar will help you develop a liking for less sweet food and a greater appreciation of the other fruity, spicy and nutty tastes involved in many cakes and desserts.

Cheese substitution

Various brands of soya cheese are available; they can be grated and sprinkled on pizza and lasagne, though they may not melt in the same way as cheddar and mozzarella do. Alternatively, nuts and tofu slices can be used to top dishes. Coating nuts or tofu lightly with olive oil will help to stop them drying out in the oven. Crumbled tofu can sometimes be used as a substitute for cheese in dishes, and in salads containing cottage cheese. To make a quiche without cheese, either use just eggs and milk/soya milk, or blend tofu with the juices from the sautéed vegetables you are putting in the quiche. Combine this fairly thick tofu mix with the other filling ingredients and omit the cheese, eggs and milk.

Salt substitution

Some medical conditions require a low or no salt diet. Lemon juice and vinegar can be used to give flavour, and other ingredients such as onions, garlic and tomato will also help bridge the flavour gap. The use of oils and salt-free butter for cooking will also help bring out flavour in the raw materials. Careful checking for added salt in tinned and processed foods is advisable. People used to a low salt diet say that although their food seems unbearably bland to begin with, after a while they start to notice the other flavours in foods more.

Nut substitution

In recent years, extreme reactions to nuts have become far more common—so much so, that most airlines no longer serve their passengers with little packets of nuts shortly after take-off, and give out little packets of savoury biscuits instead. This reaction can be quite severe, and comes in the same category as the allergy some people have to bee stings.

When it comes to substituting for nuts in recipes, it is best to check with the person who has the nut allergy. In many cases (though not all), seeds such as sunflower, pumpkin and sesame can be used as substitutes, and tahini can be used instead of peanut butter. Where the allergic reaction is very extreme, however, this may not be possible, and crumbled tofu or soya protein (TVP) can be used as an alternative protein. In many recipes you can just leave the nuts out, as they will not be the only source of protein on the menu.

Because nut allergies can provoke such serious reactions, traces of nuts in prepared foods need to be carefully checked for. Any dishes containing nuts should be clearly marked, as they are often not visible to the eye.

A further note for hosts and hostesses

Once a person with a special diet trusts you to provide the food he or she requires, you will both be able to relax and enjoy the time you spend together. It can be very annoying when people say they are (for example) 'vegan', and then poach three slices of the creamiest chocolate gateaux, but it would be unfair to tar with the same brush those people who are more committed to their diets. You often can't tell how serious people are about their diet until you have eaten with them—whatever they say. So it is important to respect special diets and take them seriously.

Just as you would never offer soup made with meat, chicken or fish stock to a vegetarian, so too it is advisable not to let forbidden ingredients creep into the foods being served to someone on a special diet. They might pass unnoticed—but, on the other hand, there might be some kind of reaction. Whether emotional or physical, this is not worth risking.

Lastly, if you have to make a special diet for a guest, there's no need to make a song and dance about it. Make it as similar to what everyone else is having as you can. Enjoy the thanks without making your guest feel too singled out. Your effort will normally be proved well worthwhile, but if you feel at all nervous about the situation, there is nothing wrong with asking a guest to bring—or cook—his or her own food!

CLOCKWISE FROM TOP LEFT:
MUSHROOM SOUP WITH SHERRY
GINGERY CARROT AND ORANGE SOUP
GREENS AND BEANS SOUP
RED ROOT SOUP

SOUPS

Vegetable Stock
Borscht
Broccoli and Buckwheat Soup
Gingery Carrot and Orange Soup
Gazpacho Toledano
Greens and Beans Soup
Leek and Potato Soup
Oh My Dhaling Lentil Soup
Miso Soup
Mushroom Soup with Sherry
Parsnip and Rosemary Soup
Red Root Soup
Sweet Potato and Fennel Soup
Fresh Tomato and Basil Soup
Chunky Vegetable Soup
Juggling with Onions

VEGETABLE STOCK

At the heart of any good soup or bean stew is the flavoursome liquid you cook it with. Just as you would save the bones of a chicken after Sunday lunch and boil them to make stock if you were a carnivore, so you need to develop the habit of saving all tender bits of cutaway vegetables to make stock. And not only this—it needs to be second nature to save the liquid you have cooked your vegetables in. Some people avoid adding brassicas (broccoli, cabbage, sprouts etc.) to stock as they find their flavour very dominating—but this really depends on the kind of soup you're making. Cabbage water might be fine in a mixed vegetable soup or minestrone, but can overpower the main flavour in, for example, a mushroom, carrot or tomato soup. However, it's always worth tasting any vegetable water you have before reaching your final verdict. It's much more energy-efficient to use liquid from vegetables you've cooked anyway than to make a special brew.

Having said that, the following recipe gives ingredients for a stock you can make from scratch, and to which you can add. A strip of the Japanese seaweed kombu contributes to the depth of flavour.

Makes 2-4 pints (1-2 litres/1-2 US quarts)	16 pints (9 litres/10 US quarts)
1 medium potato, scrubbed and cut in big chunks	3 large
1 medium white onion, peeled and halved	3 large
1-2 medium carrots, scrubbed & cut in 2" (5 cm) lengths	8 medium
1-2 sticks celery, scrubbed & cut in 2" (5 cm) lengths	1 head
2-4 cloves of garlic	12 cloves
1-2 tsp mixed dried herbs	2-4 tbsp
pinch black pepper	1 tsp
2-3 bay leaves	10
1/3 strip kombu	1 strip
approx. 2-4 pints (1-2 litres/1-2 US quarts) water	16 pints (9 litres/10 US quarts)

(Alternatively, use a similar volume of mixed vegetable trimmings, including organic potato peelings, celery leaves or base, onion tops, carrot bottoms, bean pods etc.. These can be used as a substitute for some listed vegetables, or to replace them entirely.)

1. Assemble all the ingredients in a large saucepan. Fill with fresh water, up to about 3" (8 cm) below the top of pan, to allow plenty of room for bubbling. Put a lid on and bring to the boil. Reduce heat and simmer for 1½ hours, keeping the lid slightly tilted to allow steam to escape and prevent boiling over.

2. Strain off liquid and use as required. If you are not using it immediately, allow it to cool with vegetables in, before straining through a large sieve or colander.

BORSCHT

Here is a typically Russian soup, packed with cabbage, beetroot, carrots, potatoes and celery. The combination of honey, cider vinegar and caraway gives it a delicious sweet and sour kick that is perfectly complemented by a spoonful of sour cream, dropped in the middle.

For 6-8	For 40
5 oz (140g/1 cup) thinly sliced onions	1½ lb (700g)
6 oz (170g/1 cup) thinly sliced potato	1 lb 12 oz (800g)
5 oz (140g/1 cup) thinly sliced raw beetroot	1½ lb (700g)
1 medium carrot, thinly sliced	5 medium
1 stalk celery, thinly sliced	5 stalks
6 oz (170 g/1½ cups) thinly sliced cabbage	1 lb 12 oz (800g)
2 tsp caraway seed	3 tbsp
½ tsp dill weed	3 tsp
4 tsp cider vinegar	4 fl oz (100 ml)
1 tbsp honey	4 fl oz (100 ml)
3 pints (1.7 litres/2 US quarts) stock	15 pints (8.9 litres/2¼ US gallons)
2-3 pinches salt to taste	2-3 tbsp
1-2 pinches black pepper	1-2 tsp

1. Sauté the onions with the caraway seeds and some salt in the bottom of a large soup pan.

2. When the onions are beginning to go translucent, add the celery, carrots and cabbage and cook until the cabbage is wilted.

3. Add the potatoes and stock. Simmer everything until just tender.

4. Boil the beetroot separately for about 15 minutes. Add towards end of cooking time—this will ensure that the vegetables don't all get dyed a uniform pink by the beetroot.

5. Finally, add dill, honey and vinegar. Adjust the seasoning and serve on its own, with sour cream, or with yoghurt.

BROCCOLI AND BUCKWHEAT SOUP

This wholesome, moss-coloured soup is a particular favourite of our ecologist Stephan Harding. Perhaps this is because it contains buckwheat. As a boy, Stephan had a beloved Polish Aunt who fed him on *kasha*, as buckwheat is known in Poland. Although this soup is blissfully devoid of the meaty gravy Stephan's Auntie Hanka would have stewed up her *kasha* with, it still reminds him of her enough to inspire him to sing a tuneful 'ode to broccoli soup' every time we make it! The other main ingredient, broccoli, is full of vitamin C and also a very good natural source of calcium.

For 6-10	For 35-40
1-2 large onions	3 lb (1.4 kg)
3 oz (85g/$\frac{1}{2}$ cup) buckwheat	1 lb (450g/2$\frac{1}{2}$ cups)
1 lb (450 g/5 cups) prepared broccoli	5 lb (2.3 kg)
1 tsp dried thyme	2 tbsp
1 pint (600 ml/2$\frac{1}{2}$ cups) stock	6 pints (3.5 litres/1 US gallon)
16 fl oz (450 ml/2 cups) milk	5 pints (3 litres/3 US quarts)
4 fl oz (100 ml/$\frac{1}{2}$ cup) cream or yoghurt	1 pint (600 ml/2$\frac{1}{2}$ cups)
a little olive oil/butter	a little more

1. Peel and roughly chop onions. Rinse the broccoli and begin rough chopping and floretting. Pare away the woodier outside of the lower stem. For the smaller quantity you'll need to reserve about half the florets whole. For the larger quantity, reserve a quarter of the broccoli florets whole. Set these aside.

2. Rinse buckwheat. Begin to sauté onions for 5-10 minutes in olive oil and butter.

3. As the onions begin to go slightly pearly, add the broccoli, thyme and buckwheat. Stir so that everything is coated with some of the oil/butter.

4. Add the stock (or hot water). Bring to boil and simmer for 30-40 minutes until cooked.

5. Blanch or steam reserved broccoli florets in a separate pan until they are bright green. Drain immediately.

6. Heat milk in a separate pan until steaming (but not boiling).

7. Blend the soup.

8. Turn off the heat. Stir in the milk, and cream/yoghurt. Also stir in half the pre-cooked florets. Scatter the rest of the florets on the top as a garnish when you are ready to serve the soup.

GINGERY CARROT & ORANGE SOUP

A warming and tangy soup that has a beautiful muted-orange glow, and will add a touch of spice to your day.

For 4-6	For 35-40
7 oz (200 g/1¹/₃ cups) onions, chopped	3 lb (1.4 kg)
1 lb (450 g) or 4 medium carrots	8 lb (3.6 kg)
2 sticks celery	1 head
4 oz (110 g/²/₃ cup) potatoes, chopped	1 lb 12 oz (800 g)
1 pint (600 ml/2¹/₂ cups) stock/water approx.	12-16 pints (7-9 litres/2-2¹/₂ US gallons)
1-2 tbsp grated ginger	4-5 oz (100-150 g/²/₃-1 cup)
juice of 2-3 oranges	3¹/₂ pints (2 litres/2 US quarts) orange juice
zest of ¹/₂-1 orange, if organic	zest (and juice) of 4
salt and pepper to taste	1-2 tbsp salt, 1-2 tsp pepper
olive oil to sauté	olive oil to sauté
small knob butter (optional)	large knob

1. Rough chop onions. Scrub and rough chop carrots, celery and potatoes.

2. Sauté onions and celery in oil in the bottom of a large saucepan. After a few minutes add carrots, and continue to sauté until onions are beginning to go pearly. Stir occasionally to avoid burning.

3. Stir in the potatoes, then add enough water to cover the vegetables by a couple of inches.

4. Bring to the boil, then reduce heat and simmer until the vegetables are tender.

5. Add the orange juice, zest (if using) and grated ginger.

6. Blend the soup.

7. Add more stock/hot water/orange juice to achieve desired thickness.

8. Season with salt, freshly ground black pepper, bouillon powder and a little butter.

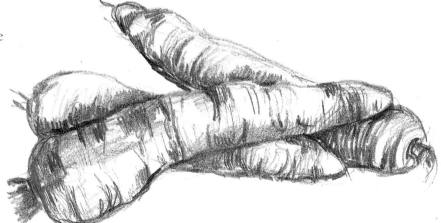

GAZPACHO TOLEDANO

In the heat of summer there can be nothing more refreshing than a cold and truly Mediterranean soup containing a delicious blend of cucumbers, tomatoes, peppers and onions. In England, of course, it is often difficult to predict which day will be sunny and which cool and cloudy—even in July. In fact I have begun to think that planning to make Gazpacho on a particular day is tempting fate. The clouds, it seems, will inevitably start homing in on the Old Postern as soon as we start peeling cucumbers. But all is not lost. Gazpacho keeps well, indeed improves, and can be brought out again when the sun emerges from the clouds.

For 6-10	For 30-40
7-8 medium red tomatoes	30 plus 2.5 kg (5½ lb) canned tomatoes
½ medium sized cucumber	3
1 green pepper	6
1 small onion	6 small, or 3 large
3 cloves garlic	12-18 cloves or 3 tbsp minced
1½ slices French bread	9 slices or 2 small 10" (25 cm) baguettes
1-3 tsp fresh coriander or basil leaves	3-5 tbsp
12 fl oz (350 ml) cold water	3½ pints (2 litres/2 US quarts)
4 tbsp white wine vinegar to taste	8 fl oz (200 ml/1 cup)
6 tbsp olive oil	8 fl oz (200 ml/1 cup)
2 tsp paprika	4 tbsp
3 tsp salt	3-4 tbsp
pinch ground cumin	2 tsp to taste
black pepper	1-2 tsp

1. Cut the tomatoes into wedges. Peel and dice the cucumbers. Mince garlic. Coarsely dice the onion. De-seed and rough chop the green peppers to similar size. (As all vegetables will be blended, they need not be sliced very small.)

2. Combine vegetables (including canned chopped tomatoes, if making the large quantity) with the cubed French bread and the water. Blend with a rod blender or in a liquidizer until smooth, or to the texture you desire.

3. Add the finely chopped fresh herbs, oil and wine vinegar, and whisk until well mixed. Season with paprika, salt, freshly ground cumin and freshly ground black pepper.

4. Chill in fridge and then serve. On a really hot day, a few ice cubes maybe added as a final embellishment.

GREENS AND BEANS SOUP

This simple, nutritious, farmhouse soup can be made with any kind of white bean and leafy green vegetable. It can be served with a hunk of bread, and, if you like, a sprinkling of grated cheese. Once standard peasant fare in many parts of rural Spain, it is now popular in the most sophisticated vegetarian restaurants of the big city, where it brings a touch of rustic countryside comfort to the cut and thrust of urban existence.

For 6-10	For 40
8 oz (225 g/1¼ cups) butter beans or haricots	3 lb (1.4 kg)
½ strip kombu (if available)	1 strip
1-2 bay leaves	6-10
pinch dried sage + 2 tsp chopped fresh sage	2 tsp dried + 4 tsp fresh
2 tsp chopped fresh parsley	4 tbsp
1-2 cloves garlic, fine sliced	6-12 cloves
8 oz onion (225 g/1½ cups), sliced	3 lb (1.4 kg)
2-3 stalks celery	1 head
6 oz (175 g/3 cups) greens, shredded (see 5 below)	2 lb (900 g)
1½ pints (900 ml/1 US quart) boiling water for blanching	8 pints (4.5 litres/5 US quarts)
butter/olive oil for frying	butter/olive oil for frying
salt and black pepper	salt and black pepper
1-2 tsp vegetable stock powder to taste (optional)	2-4 tbsp

1. Soak the beans overnight in three times their depth of water. Next day, place the beans and their soaking water in a soup pot with enough extra water or stock to ensure they are still well covered. Add bay leaves and dried sage. Cook beans until tender (1 to 2 hours).

2. Remove quarter to one third of the beans and blend. Either blend until completely smooth, or allow to remain quite coarsely blended. Recombine with the whole beans. (Alternatively, mash the beans a bit using a potato masher.) Next fry the onions, celery and garlic in butter/oil until soft and transparent. Add to the soup pot.

3. Suitable greens are, for example, kale, spring greens and savoy cabbage. Courgette slices, purple sprouting broccoli or calabrese could also be included. Wash and shred them into ribbons ½" (1-2 cm) wide. Finely slice tender part of stem. Fifteen minutes before serving, blanch briefly in boiling water. Drain and keep the blanching water.

4. Add the greens and chopped fresh sage to the soup and continue to simmer if necessary, until the greens are tender but still bright green. Add as much reserved blanching water as necessary to give the desired consistency. This is not intended to be a very thick soup, and should have more the consistency of a pond in which the mud has been churned up by a bathing buffalo.

5. Taste and adjust seasoning as necessary. Stir in half the freshly chopped parsley and garnish with the rest.

LEEK AND POTATO SOUP

Throughout the English winter we are sustained by leeks. They go on arriving from Dartington's organic market garden long after potatoes and carrots have given up growing for the season.

Here is one of our favourite ways of using leeks: a delicious and satisfying soup, which can be made as chunky or as smooth as you like. Elegantly nicknamed the 'vichyssoise' of vegetable soups, it can be served with cheese, and fresh bread rolls still warm from the oven. The perfect antidote to cold fingers and toes!

For 4-6	For 35-40
10 oz (300 g/3 cups) leeks, when prepared	$4^{1}/_{2}$ lb (2 kg) when prepared
5 oz (150 g/$^{3}/_{4}$ cup) onions, diced	2 lb (900 g)
9 oz (250 g/$1^{1}/_{2}$ cups) potatoes, diced	4 lb (1.8 kg)
1-2 stalks celery	1 head
2-3 tbsp chopped parsley	6 oz (170 g/$2^{1}/_{2}$ cups)
$1^{1}/_{2}$ pints (800 ml/1 US quart) veg. stock or water	10 pints (5.7 litres/$1^{1}/_{2}$ US gallons)
6 fl oz (150 ml/$^{3}/_{4}$ cup) milk*	2 pints (1 litre/5 cups)
5-7 tbsp cream*	1 pint (600 ml/$2^{1}/_{2}$ cups)
1-2 pinches salt	1-3 tbsp
pinch freshly ground black pepper	1 tsp to taste
1 tsp vegetable stock powder, if available	2 tbsp
1 tsp Dijon mustard	2 tbsp
olive oil/butter to sauté	olive oil/butter to sauté
*vegan substitute for milk and cream:	
15 fl oz (400 ml/2 cups) warmed soya milk	3 pints (1.7 litres/2 US quarts)

1. Peel and dice the onions into fairly small pieces. Scrub the potatoes, remove any bad bits and cut into smallish slices or dice. Slice the celery finely. With the leeks, remove browning or tough leaves but try and use as much of the green as possible. Cut off root tip, slice up the middle and chop—again, the desired size is quite small, so that a medley of different vegetable pieces can happily intermingle on your soup spoon. After slicing, put the leeks into a bowl of cold water and wash thoroughly to remove any soil. Drain, using a colander.

2. Sauté onions in the bottom of your soup saucepan, using a little olive oil or oil/butter combination. Continue until they are beginning to go transparent. Do not brown.

3. Add the celery, leeks and potatoes, and stir well.

4. Add enough of the liquid to cover the vegetables. Bring to the boil. Reduce heat and simmer until they are tender.

5. Blending: we normally remove about half the vegetables and blend those remaining in the saucepan with a hand-held blender, then recombine. Sometimes we blend the lot.

6. Add more stock or water to give the almost desired consistency—remember that if you are going to add cream or milk this will make the soup a bit runnier. Add the milk or cream towards the end, but do not boil the soup once you've added it, as this may cause the cream to separate. If you're adding a lot of milk, carefully re-heat soup until almost boiling—or heat the milk in a separate pan and then add. If using soya milk, it is even more important to heat it separately before adding, as it has an even greater tendency to curdle when boiled in soup.

7. Season to taste with salt, pepper, vegetable stock powder or cubes, and mustard. Stir most of the chopped parsley into the soup. Sprinkle the rest on top.

A 'Living Machine'
created by participants on
John and Nancy Jack Todd's course,
June 2000

OH MY DHALING LENTIL SOUP

Once upon a time Satish Kumar, the college's Director of Programmes and Editor of *Resurgence* magazine, used to make oceans of excess dhal every week. This provided the basis of a very warming and nutritious soup that people found quite lovely. In fact, lentil soup became so popular that we soon had to find ways of re-creating it even when there was no leftover dhal to dally with. This recipe is the result.

For 5-7	For 35-40
8 oz (220 g/1¼ cups) onions, diced	3 lb (1.4 kg)
2 stalks celery, chopped finely	1 head celery
8 oz carrots (220 g/1½ cups), diced	3 lb (1.4 kg)
5 oz tomatoes (150 g/½ cup), chopped small	2 lb (900 g)
4 tbsp fresh herbs, chopped	2-3 oz (60 g/1 cup)
5 oz (140 g/¾ cup) red lentils	1¾ lb (800 g)
or ¾ pints (about 2 cups) leftover dhal	or 8 pints dhal (3.4 litres/5 US quarts)
½ tsp cumin seed	1 tbsp
salt and pepper to taste	to taste

1. Sauté the onions, carrots and celery in olive oil in the bottom of a large soup saucepan, until the onions are beginning to go transparent. Add the cumin seed during this process (not necessary if you are using dhal, as it already has cumin in it).

2. Add the tomatoes and red lentils and just enough stock/water to generously cover the ingredients by 2-3 inches. Simmer until the carrots are tender and the lentils swelled and soft.

3. If using leftover dhal, add this when the carrots are tender. It does not matter that there will be more onions and tomatoes in the version made with this.

4. Blend the soup with a rod blender until smooth—or keep chunky if you prefer. Dilute with extra water to achieve desired consistency—usually quite thick.

5. Season with salt, pepper and stock powder/cubes. Add a knob of butter for extra richness if you like—and finally the chopped fresh herbs: parsley, sage, rosemary and thyme. . . .

MISO SOUP

Miso is a thick, salty, brown paste made with fermented brown rice or barley. It comes in many varieties, and its texture varies from very smooth to coarse. When diluted with water, it becomes a delicious, easily digested soup that is ideal when convalescing. In Japan, miso is a staple ingredient in most savoury dishes. Miso soup itself is prepared in many different ways, each region often having its own distinctive style. Sometimes potatoes, carrots, leeks and other vegetables are added to give a wholesome vegetable soup. Other times, as in this simple recipe, just a sprinkling of spring onion, radish, tofu and wakame are added to discreetly embellish the liquid miso. As with so much of Japanese cooking, full use is made of the rich tastes offered by dried seaweeds—of which kombu and wakame are fine examples.

For 4-6	For 30
half strip of kombu	3 strips
4 tbsp miso	18 fl oz (510 ml/2¼ cups) approx.
4 oz (110 g) tofu, small cubes	2 lb (900 g)
2 spring onions, small rings	16
3-4 cherry radishes, thin rings	4-6 oz (150 g) or 15-20 radishes
1½ pints (850 ml/3½ cups) water	12 pints (7 litres/7½ US quarts)
½ strip wakame, narrow strips (optional)	3 strips

1. Simmer the kombu in boiling water for 20-30 minutes. Remove kombu.

2. Add miso and stir until dissolved. Add cubed tofu and wakame strips. (The wakame strips can be cut with either a sharp knife or scissors). Simmer for 5 minutes.

3. Remove any old and discoloured outer leaves from the spring onion, then cut up into small ¼" (½ cm) rings, discarding root. Use as much of the green as possible. Minimally top and tail the radishes and cut in thin slices that will float.

4. When serving time arrives, stir half the spring onion and radish into the hot soup—and garnish its surface with the rest.

MUSHROOM SOUP WITH SHERRY

Mushroom soup gourmets will adore this silky-rich liquid, densely populated with delicious pieces of mushroom. We normally use open organic chestnut mushrooms for fullness of flavour. The cream and sherry can be added at your own discretion!

For 4-6	For 35-40
1 lb 5 oz (600 g) mushrooms, sliced	8 lb (3.6 kg)
4 oz (110 g/¾ cup) potatoes, small cubes	1½ lb (700 g)
8 oz (225 g/1½ cups) onions, sliced	3 lb (1.4 kg)
2 sticks celery, chopped	1 head celery
1 smallish leek, sliced	4 leeks
1 pint (600 ml/2½ cups) water	6 pints (3.4 litre/1 US gallon)
4 fl oz (100 ml/½ cup) medium sherry	½-1 pint (300-600 ml/1¼-2½ cups)
5-7 fl oz (200 ml/½-1 cup) single cream	2 pints (1 litre/5 cups)
pinch salt, to taste	1-3 tbsp
freshly ground black pepper	1-2 tsp
vegetable stock powder (bouillon)	1-3 tbsp
olive oil for sautéeing	olive oil for sautéeing
1-2 tsp chopped parsley for garnish	3-4 tbsp

1. Sauté onions, celery and leeks in olive oil in a large saucepan, until they begin to go transparent. This can be done in the bottom of a saucepan large enough to eventually hold all the soup. Stir in the potatoes, and then add the water or stock. Continue to cook until all the vegetables are soft. Blend.

2. Meanwhile, sauté the mushrooms separately in olive oil. When the mushrooms have particularly huge stalks, I break them off before chopping, and cook them with the onions etc., so they get blended. With the large quantity, it will probably take you 2-3 goes to sauté all the mushrooms, depending on your pan size. If the mushrooms seem to be absorbing an inordinate amount of olive oil, add some water to help with the cooking-without-sticking process.

3. Add the sautéed mushrooms and their juices to the blended mixture. Season. Before serving, add sherry and cream. Add more water if necessary to achieve desired consistency. Do not boil the soup once the cream is added, as it may curdle. Garnish with freshly chopped parsley and attractively arranged slices of raw mushroom.

JUGGLING WITH ONIONS

Many people who come to Schumacher College bring ideas about how to chop onions without shedding tears. These range from the sublime to the ridiculous: onion tears are, it seems, a problem that unites people the world over. There are other people—at least one on every course—who have rather contrary ideas. They claim that it is actually very OK to sob with onions. Thank God for such participants! They eagerly volunteer to slice the onions every week because they believe it will be a cleansing experience. "Please let me slice them by hand," they say. "No! No! I don't want to wear goggles. Blow out the candle. I want to cry."

Whether onion-tears are welcome or not, they are always an occasion for bonding amongst group members. Invariably, seeing each other shedding onion-tears is a great excuse for lavishing huge amounts of sympathy all round. Soon everyone is hugging each other. Cooking is abandoned for a few minutes, while the group process surreptitiously imbues the menu with its own richness.

Mirth and masochism aside, here are ten tips for tear-free onion slicing, gathered over the first ten years of the college's life. I recommend a combination of the last four if you want to achieve genuine dry-eyed success with a huge pile of onions—and a combination of the first 5 if you merely want distraction!

1. Balance a peeled onion on your head. (You are allowed to cut the end off.)

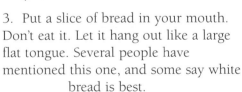

2. Stick two used matches between your teeth, with The sulphurous brown ends in the room.

3. Put a slice of bread in your mouth. Don't eat it. Let it hang out like a large flat tongue. Several people have mentioned this one, and some say white bread is best.

4. Light a candle.

5. Light a stick of incense.

6. Open a window.

7. Wear a pair of swimming goggles to protect your eyes.

8. Cover the unpeeled onions with cold water. Once peeled, place the peeled onions in cold water before you slice them.

9. Cut the root off last. This is where all the noxious fumes emanate from.

10. Wear contact lenses!

CLOCKWISE FROM TOP LEFT:
CHEESE, CASHEW & WALNUT ROAST
SPINACH & MUSHROOM PLAIT
COLOURFUL STIR FRY WITH TEMPEH
SAVOURY VEGETABLE TART WITH RICH WALNUT CRUST
AUBERGINE ROLL-UPS

MAIN COURSE DISHES

Aubergine Roll-ups

Stuffed Aubergines

Satish's Indian Bhojan

Broccoli & Red Pepper Quiche

Roast Vegetable Tart with Rich Walnut Crust

Spinach & Mushroom Plait

Spinach Borek Triangles

Tangy Turtle Beans

Solomon's Stew

Hilary's Red Red Red Chilli

Lentil Shepherd's Pie

Herby Scalloped Potatoes with Smoked Cheese

Walnut & Mushroom Bolognese

Ratatouille Lasagne

No Frills Classic Macaroni Cheese

Penne with Pesto, Red Pepper & Mushroom

Cheese, Cashew & Walnut Roast with Sherry Sauce

Savoury Vegetable Crumble

Wendy Cook's Polenta Pie

Sij's Spicy Stuffed Peppers with Tantalizing Sauces

Slow Pizza

Tricolor Rice

Tofu & Broccoli in Peanut Sauce

Tofu Marinade (served cold)

Colourful Stir Fry with Tempeh

AUBERGINE ROLL-UPS

This is a very decorative way of serving aubergines (eggplants). It's quite fiddly to make, as the creation of many individual small rolls is involved. However this dish can be prepared in advance and reheated. I often prepare and roast the aubergine slices with a group in the morning, and also put together the stuffing in advance. By supper time, the only thing left is to roll up the aubergine around a few spoonfuls of stuffing.

For 6	For 40
3 oz (85 g/⅔ cup) cashew pieces	1¼ lb (600 g)
1¼ oz (½ cup) organic soya mince (TVP)	9 oz (250 g/3½ cups)
4 large aubergines	28
2 tbsp tomato purée (paste)	7 fl oz (200 ml)
3 medium tomatoes	20
half a medium red pepper	4
one smallish onion	7 approx.
1-2 tbsp fresh chopped basil	3 oz (85 g/1½ cups)
pinch dried oregano	2 tsp
2 tsp Dijon mustard	4-5 tbsp
2-3 pinches salt & pinch black pepper	2-3 tbsp salt & 1-2 tsp pepper (to taste)
4 oz (110 g/½ cup) goat's cheese approx.	2 lb (900 g) approx.

1. Begin by preparing the aubergines. Slice these lengthwise into ¼" (6 mm) sheets the full width and length of the vegetable. Reserve the smaller side pieces for the filling. Lay the other sheets of aubergine next to each other on some baking parchment on top of a baking tray. Paint these with olive oil on both sides. Sprinkle lightly with salt and bake in a moderate oven for 20-30 minutes until cooked but not brown. Meanwhile begin to dice the aubergine sides, onions, tomato, and red pepper quite finely. Begin to sauté these in olive oil with the oregano.

2. Pour boiling water on to the soya protein, just covering it. Leave it to expand for ten minutes or so, then tip into a sieve and drain off any surplus water, pressing lightly with a wooden spoon. If you do not like soya protein, substitute with brown breadcrumbs or brown rice.

3. Add the tomato purée to the sauteed vegetables and cook for a few more minutes. Next add the cashew pieces and soya protein. Stir thoroughly and cook a little more. Add the fresh basil. Season with salt, freshly ground black pepper and Dijon mustard. Allow to cool.

4. To make the roll-ups, place a large spoonful of stuffing at one end of an aubergine slice. Roll the aubergine over the stuffing, and place with the overlapping end downwards in an ovenproof baking dish, so that the rolls are touching and supporting each other. Place small strips of goat's cheese (or mozzarella or cheddar) on the top of each roll.

5. Bake in a moderate oven (180°C, 350°F, gas mark 4) for 25-35 minutes until hot through, with the cheese melted and perhaps slightly browning. Serve with fresh green salad and rice. The recipe should produce 2-4 roll-ups each.

STUFFED AUBERGINES

Nowadays the polytunnels at Dartington produce glossy purple aubergines (eggplant) every summer. This gives us a wonderful excuse to adopt a typically Turkish menu and still feel we're being bioregional!

For 4-6	For 30
2 lb (1 kg) or 3-4 medium-sized aubergines	10 lb (4.6 kg)
6 oz (170 g/1 cup) onions, finely chopped	3 lb (1.4 kg)
4 cloves garlic, crushed	4 tbsp crushed
3-4 tbsp pine nuts or cashews	8 oz (225 g/2 cups)
8 oz (225 g/1 cup) chopped fresh tomatoes	2½ lb (1.1 kg)
2 tbsp finely chopped parsley	1½ oz (45 g/¾ cup)
2 tbsp finely chopped basil	1½ oz (45 g/¾ cup)
4 tbsp whole parmesan, grated	3½ oz (100 g/1½ cups)
1½ oz (40 g/½ cup) fresh brown breadcrumbs	5 oz (140 g/1⅔ cups)
6 oz (170 g/1½ cups) mozzarella or cheddar	2 lb (700 g)
salt and pepper to taste	1 tsp pepper, 2-3 tsp salt

1. Halve the aubergines lengthwise. The stalk can be removed or left on for effect. Paint aubergines with olive oil and place with cut face down on some baking parchment or an oiled baking tray. Bake in oven for 20-30 minutes until beginning to turn bronze and soft. When cool, scoop out the flesh leaving a ¼" (½ cm) thick shell. Chop up the aubergine flesh you have collected.

2. Fry the onions and garlic in olive oil until beginning to go transparent. Add the chopped fresh tomatoes and herbs and sauté some more. Then add the chopped aubergines and pine nuts/cashews. Season with freshly ground black pepper and salt. Cook for a further 15 minutes and remove from heat. After allowing to cool a little, add the breadcrumbs and parmesan. Check seasoning.

3. Fill the aubergine shells with the mixture. Heap up a little if necessary, and press the mixture securely but gently into the shells with the back of a metal spoon or your clean hands.

4. Bake in an oiled ovenproof dish at 180°C (350°F, gas mark 4) for 30 minutes, then top with sliced mozzarella or grated cheddar cheese. Continue to cook for a further 15-20 minutes until the cheese is developing golden brown patches.

5. Serve with (for example) a tomato sauce or salsa, green salad and either rice, new potatoes or tabbouleh.

SATISH'S INDIAN BHOJAN

Satish Kumar, our Director of Programmes, is unusual amongst Indian men of his generation in that his mother brought him up not only to cook, but to enjoy spending many happy hours in the kitchen. This he continues to do whilst at Schumacher College, and participants often feel delighted when they discover they are in the Monday night cooking group and will have the mysteries of North Indian cooking calmly revealed to them under the tutelage of Satish and his giant sauté pans. For many more traditional men from the subcontinent, their first encounter with cooking in the Schumacher College kitchen is met with a mixture of trepidation and eager anticipation. Indeed, they have often asked me to take a snapshot for their wives, as evidence that this unlikely occasion has really taken place!

Before proceeding with the recipes, over to Satish for one of the most essential ingredients—atmosphere.

"My first memory of cooking in my mother's kitchen takes me back to the age of five. I was making chappatis—unleavened flat bread. I loved playing with the dough and rolling it out. All sorts of shapes would emerge—and my mother would laugh at my triangular chappatis, knowing they should have been round.

"Our kitchen was a warm and reviving place, that brought all who cooked there immediately in touch with earth and fire—those basic elements that underlie all cooking, yet are so often invisible in modern kitchens. My mother sat on the ground, cross-legged. Around her sat her children, and everything she needed. Between us, pots and pans bubbled on a brick and mud stove. Two or three logs fed the flame, pointing towards the chimney where the smoke disappeared.

"We were a family of eight brothers and sisters—four boys and four girls. Mother insisted that all four boys learned to cook. This was exceptional, but she believed that if you can enjoy cooking, you can enjoy eating even more.

"Mother was an intuitive cook and we learned by observing how she prepared the food. She never had any recipe books—there were none in the house. In any case, Mother could not read or write, but she was herself a book of countless recipes.

"When I became a monk I stopped cooking, and so from the age of nine to eighteen the practice of cooking lapsed. Later, when I joined a Gandhian Ashram, Mother's cooking came back to me very quickly. I met a man called Sundarani, for whom cooking was a creative process, an art form. He was also a gardener and produced many kinds of vegetables and herbs. So there at the Ashram I truly experienced the joy of cooking. I liked to do nothing more than work in the garden, pick the vegetables, wash them, chop them finely, use appropriate combinations, appropriate herbs and spices, and take pleasure in serving the food and also in washing up. Cooking at the Ashram became a form of spiritual work, a form of meditation, a form of service—and a form of aesthetic experience."

The following gives all you will need for Satish's classic Indian meal (or bhojan), consisting of several different dishes. A few pickles, such as mango, brinjal and lime, are often served as well. The level of spiciness has been tailored for mild Western palates, and can be zapped up if you prefer your curries hotter. In the individual recipes which follow, the smaller and larger quantities are separated by an oblique (/), as usual.

For 4-6	For 40
1 lb (450 g/3 cups) potatoes in $\frac{1}{2}$"(1$\frac{1}{2}$ cm) cubes	7 lb (3.2 kg)
1$\frac{1}{2}$ lb (700 g/1 medium-sized) cauliflower cut into little florets	10 lb (4.5 kg/6 or 7 medium caulis)
12 oz (350 g/2$\frac{1}{2}$ cups) onions, thin sliced	6 lb (2.6 kg)
10 oz (275 g/1$\frac{1}{4}$ cups) chopped tomatoes	4 lb (1.8 kg)
4$\frac{1}{2}$ oz (125 g/$\frac{2}{3}$ cup) red split lentils	2 lb (900 g)
3 oz (85 g/$\frac{3}{4}$ cup) frozen peas	1 bag (1 lb 2 oz/500 g)
9 oz (250 g) spinach	4$\frac{1}{2}$ lb (2 kg)
14 oz (400 g/2 cups) basmati rice	6 lb (2.8 kg)
4 oz (110 g) natural yoghurt	2 lb (900 g)
2-3" (5-7 cm) cucumber	1
1-2 oz (30-55 g/$\frac{1}{2}$-1 cup) fresh coriander leaves	6-12 oz (200-400 g/3-6 cups)
4-6 cloves garlic, minced	1-2 heads
1-2 oz (30-55 g/2-4 tbsp) fresh ginger root, grated	4-8 oz (100-200 g/1 cup)
1-2 green chillies (depending on strength)	4-8
2 tbsp turmeric	3 oz (85 g/$\frac{2}{3}$ cup)
2 tbsp garam masala	3 oz (85 g/$\frac{2}{3}$ cup)
2-3 tsp cumin seed	4-6 tbsp
$\frac{1}{2}$ lemon approx.	2
salt to taste	to taste
poppadums—allow one each and a few extra	

Cover the bases of three average/large frying pans with olive oil. Use large saucepans if large frying pans or sauté pans are not available. Gently fry 2 tsp/2 tbsp cumin seed in each until brown. Add one third of the onions to each pan and fry slowly until golden brown. Cooking these onions separately like this is the first stage in making the following three dishes (Saag Aloo, Ghobi Mutter and Dhal).

Saag Aloo (potatoes and spinach)

When making the larger quantity, it is best to pre-cook the potatoes in some boiling water until soft but not breaking up (15-20 minutes). For the smaller quantity this isn't really necessary. To one pan add the par-boiled potatoes and 2 tsp/2 tbsp ginger, 1 tbsp/4 tbsp garlic, 2 tsp/3 tbsp turmeric, 1 tbsp/4 tbsp garam masala, $\frac{1}{2}$ tsp/2 tbsp salt. Meanwhile steam a quantity of spinach leaf and then add to the potatoes about 5 minutes before serving. Alternatively, use defrosted frozen spinach that has been thawing for several hours, preferably overnight.

Ghobi Mutter (Cauliflower and peas)

To another pan of golden brown onions add 1 tbsp/4 tbsp garam masala, 2 tsp/3 tbsp turmeric, ½ tbsp/2 tbsp salt and the cauliflower. Stir well and cook, covered, over a low flame until tender. Using plenty of oil and a lid, Satish seems to have no problem getting the cauliflower to cook. However, he suggests you add a sprinkling of water if the cauliflower is not cooking or you prefer to use less oil. Add the peas about 5-10 minutes before serving—using defrosted (or fresh) peas and adding them only towards the end of cooking time should ensure they remain bright green in colour, twinkling like emeralds on the serving table. That is how Satish likes them, though other Indian visitors have challenged him, saying curried peas should be allowed to turn khaki!

Dhal and Chonked Dhal

Sort the lentils carefully by spreading a little at a time on a white plate. Brown lentils are OK, but tiny stones are not, and though they may be very rare, they are worth checking for—for the sake of someone's tooth! Cook the lentils in three times their volume of water with ¾ tsp/2 tbsp turmeric, 1 tsp/3 tbsp garam masala and ½ tsp/4 tsp salt. When nearly cooked, add the third quantity of cooked onions and cumin and continue to simmer. Blend until creamy with a hand whisk or rod blender.

You now have the option of making 'Chonk' (or 'Tarka') dhal, but bear in mind that it requires great care and is best learned by observation. Basically, you add some cumin that has been browned in a pool of olive oil, in a small pan. While the olive oil is still piping hot and smoking you pour it into the dhal. Because it will steam up and sizzle terrifically you need to use the lid of the pan as a shield to protect your face, and you need to close the lid over the handle of the small pan you are emptying into the dhal, whilst the steam subsides. When the smoke has gone you can stir the dhal. If you are unclear about these instructions, avoid chonking. Whether chonked or not, you can go on to add the tomatoes to the dhal for the last ten minutes of cooking.

Raita

Peel and chop the cucumber. Mix with the yoghurt and a little salt. Add a little water, milk or cream to make the curd smoother—this may represent about one-eighth of the total volume, though of course it depends on the thickness of the yoghurt. Bruise some cumin seeds between your hands and scatter over the yoghurt mixture.

Another way of making raita is to include freshly chopped tomato and red onion alongside the cucumber and other ingredients.

Coriander Chutney

Wash and dry the coriander. Remove any tough stalks. Chop up the green chilli and remove seeds (unless you are going for a very hot chutney). Blend 1/4 green chillies, with the coriander leaf, 1 tbsp/4 tbsp chopped ginger, 1 tbsp/4 tbsp roughly chopped garlic, the juice of 1/2/2 lemons and about 1/4/1 tsp salt together in a food processor or liquidizer with enough olive oil to slightly thicken it (2 tbsp/8 tbsp approx.). Add a little yoghurt if you like. Traditionally, the coriander leaf would be crushed between two stones. Alternatively, a pestle and mortar could be used, or a mezzaluna—and some persistence!

For a hotter version, use double the number of chillies and omit the coriander and ginger. Red chillies can also be used.

Basmati Rice

Bring rice to the boil in the water. The ratio required is one part rice to two parts water. Once boiling, turn the burner down as low as possible and put a lid on. Continue to cook for about 15 minutes until all the water is absorbed and the rice fluffy, and grains (hopefully) still separate.

Poppadums

We always use Lijjat poppadums, which are made by a Women's Cooperative in Bombay. Fry them in about 1/4" (1/2-1 cm) of sunflower oil on both sides. Using tongs, move the papad from surface to surface several times quite swiftly—until they are light brown, puffed and rather moon-like! Hold above the frying pan with the tongs for a few seconds to shake off excess oil. Stack upright in a dish lined with absorbent paper underneath to soak up excess oil. Keep warm until serving time, if necessary.

BROCCOLI & RED PEPPER QUICHE

The original French 'Quiche Lorraine' contained eggs, cream and bacon. Sautéed onions were added later, giving an 'Alsacienne' quiche. Nowadays this open tart with a pastry crust and a filling of eggs, milk, cheese and vegetables has become a standard item for any vegetarian lunch menu. Once baked, it can be served warm or cold. It takes a little bit of preparation, but will always seem special.

For people avoiding dairy, margarine and soya milk can be used as substitutes for butter and milk, and the cheese can be left out. Other cooking options will be mentioned as the recipe unfolds.

For 1 x 11½" flan tin	For 4 x 11½" flan tins
Pastry/Dough	
13 oz (400 g/2⅔ cups) plain flour	3 lb 4 oz (500 g)
6 oz (170 g/1½ sticks) butter	1½ lb (700 g)
3 tbsp sunflower oil	5 fl oz (150 ml/½ cup)
pinch salt	2-3 tsp
a little milk or water to bind	a little bit more
Filling	
florets from 1 lb (500 g) broccoli	from 4 lb (1.8 kg)
1 large red pepper	4
12 oz (340/2 cups) sliced onions	3 lb (1.4 kg)
8 oz (220 g/2 cups) grated cheddar cheese	2 lb (900 g)
or 4 oz (120 g/1 cup) each of	or 1 lb (450 g) each
cheddar and cottage cheese	
4 tbsp fresh chopped parsley	8 fl oz (250 ml)
or 1 tbsp dried herbes de Provence	or 4 tbsp
15 fl oz (450 ml/2 cups) milk	3 pints (1.7 litres)
10 eggs	40 eggs
2 tsp Dijon mustard	2-3 tbsp
salt and pepper to taste	to taste

1. To make the pastry, slice butter into flour and salt. Break up further with a wooden spatula and then crumble with fingertips until a breadcrumb-like consistency is achieved. Bind together with the liquids to achieve a firm but springy dough.

2. Oil the tins. We normally use French flan tins with removable bottoms and fluted edges. Then divide the dough up so that you have as many dough-balls as tins. Carefully roll each piece out to approx. ⅛" (2-3mm) thick on a floured table top. Roll lightly around a rolling pin and carefully unroll over the flan tin, gently easing

into the 'corners'. Trim pastry case with a knife so that it stands just a few millimetres above the edge of the tin (it will sink slightly). Patch with surplus pastry as necessary—water or milk can be used as a glue. Flute edges of pastry, if you like.

3. Now you have the option of pre-baking (blind baking) the pastry case, to ensure that the crust-bottom will not be soggy. This can be done as follows. Use aluminium foil to create a supportive inner lining to keep up the walls of the pastry. Press the crumpled edges of the foil into the shape of the pastry case. Prick the base through the foil with a fork to prevent it rising up, and weigh it down with some baking peas/dry beans if you have them. Pre-bake for 15-20 minutes in a moderate to low oven, or until the pastry has become quite firm and matt, but is not yet browning. Remove the foil/beans, and if the base still looks raw return to a low oven for a few more minutes so it can continue to cook without the foil impeding its drying out. Frankly, you can still create a delicious quiche if you bypass this stage and bake your quiche all in one go. I have never had complaints and do not find a slightly moister pastry bottom unpleasant, but go for pre-baking the case if you've plenty of time and are aiming for perfection.

4. Now for the filling. Again, you can cut corners. I have often put raw vegetables into a raw pastry case when in a hurry or wanting to cut down on oil. The quiche will still be good, but definitely more watery. Traditionally, you should go for a little pre-cooking as follows. Lightly fry the onions and red peppers until beginning to soften (5-10 minutes). Remove from heat.

5. Blanch the broccoli florets in boiling salted water and strain. They should be bright green and still a little crispy. (All the leftover stalks and stem can go towards a soup.)

6. Whisk together the milk, eggs and mustard. Then spoon the vegetables into the pastry cases, putting an equal amount into each. Sprinkle salt, pepper, parsley and cheese over the vegetables.

7. Make sure the quiches are already on the baking sheets they will sit on in the oven, then pour the egg and milk mixture over the vegetables. Dip your clean fingers into the mixture and use them to jiggle together the ingredients a bit. You could do this when the quiches are still only two-thirds full; one tip to avoid them spilling over on the way to the oven is to fill them only partially to begin with, and then pour the rest of the milk and egg into the cases when they are already in the oven, sitting on an oven rack that you have pulled out and can then gently push back in. Some people prefer to mix all the filling ingredients together before adding them to the pastry cases. Experiment and find what suits you. A few pumpkin seeds tossed over the top is sometimes rather decorative as a sort of pre-cook garnish.

8. Bake for 45-60 minutes at 180°C (350°F, gas mark 4). Check after 20 minutes. Move around as necessary to ensure crust cooks evenly. The quiche is ready when the egg has set, fusing milk, cheese and vegetables together. The filling will have turned a delicious golden brown and have risen a bit—it'll feel springy when touched, but not really wobbly.

9. Serve with salads, potatoes, rice, etc., depending on how hungry you are.

SPINACH BOREK TRIANGLES

In the beginning, spinach borek was square, not triangular. This was in its Gunseli Tamcok phase. Gunseli arrived at the college on Jonathon Porritt's first course, eager to introduce her fellow participants to Turkish cuisine. One Sunday she created a large rectangular slab of borek that was cut into squares, crispy on top, deliciously dark green and mushy below. She accompanied this with a tzatziki so rich with garlic that some people claimed their dreams were altered.

Later, Patricia Shaw arrived on James Hillman's first course. In memory of her Turkish grandmother she also spent a Sunday cooking—this time folding borek triangles. We were so impressed that we asked her to teach Anne and Hilary the technique. Having become masters in the origami of cooking, there was nothing to prevent them passing the knowledge on to participants, and spinach borek parcels quickly became a feature of Friday night suppers. Serve with a colourful Greek salad and creamy tzatziki.

For 10 boreks	For 40 boreks
500 g (1 lb 1 oz) filo pastry/dough	2 kg (4^1/$_2$ lb)
3 lb (1.4 kg) spinach	12 lb (5.4 kg)
2 red peppers	8 red peppers
4 oz (110 g/^{1}/$_2$ cup) ricotta cheese	1 lb (450 g)
4 oz (110 g/^{1}/$_2$ cup) cottage cheese	1 lb (450 g)
2 oz (55 g/^{1}/$_4$ cup) feta cheese	9 oz (250 g)
2 oz (55 g/^{1}/$_2$ stick) butter	9 oz (250 g)
2 good sized onions	8
1 tsp nutmeg	3-4 tsp
salt and pepper to taste	1-2 tbsp of each approx.
optional addition: 2-3 tbsp pine nuts	4 oz (110 g/1 cup) pine nuts
vegan substitutes:	
8 oz tofu (instead of cheeses)	2 lb (900 g)
3-4 fl oz (100 ml/^{1}/$_2$ cup) olive oil approx. (instead of butter)	12 fl oz (350 ml/1^1/$_2$ cups) approx.

1.   If using frozen spinach, remove from your freezer the night before and allow to thaw out. Filo pastry can also be taken out at this stage and put in the fridge (read instructions on pack for defrosting methods. Avoid removing packaging before ready to handle pastry, as it can dry out).

2.   Tip defrosted spinach into a colander, and allow to drain. Press down with clean hands to squeeze out excess liquid. Allow to stand dripping whilst you continue with the onions. Allow the defrosted filo to come to room temperature.

3. If using fresh spinach, wash and shred. The stalk, if not too stringy, can be chopped finely and included in the mixture. Steam the spinach until it wilts but is still a vibrant green. It does not need to be completely cooked, but should be encouraged to do most of its shrinking at this stage. Allow to cool and drain off excess liquid.

4. Peel and finely slice the onions. Dice the red peppers.

5. Begin to sauté the onions in olive oil. When they have been sizzling away merrily for a few minutes, add the red pepper and continue to cook until both are soft and the pepper just tender. Combine with the drained frozen spinach, or cooled fresh spinach.

6. Given that the total vegetable mixture is now either coolish or only slightly warm, you can crumble in the feta and ricotta and stir in the cottage cheese. Also add the nutmeg, pine nuts (if you are opting for this luxurious extra), salt and pepper. For the vegan version you'll need to crumble in the tofu instead of the cheese. Stir well. (For convenience, this part can all be done in advance.)

7. Now the fiddly bit begins. Melt the butter on a low flame. Remove filo pastry from bag and gently unroll. You should, with luck, have approximately ten sheets of semi-transparent, ivory-coloured parchment. Back in the days when people made their own filo pastry, it is rumoured that a girl was ready for marriage when her beloved could read a newspaper through her pastry! Does this explain the declining popularity of marriage? In any case, beware of tricky filo that has mysteriously got too wet and wants to stick to itself. This doesn't happen often, but when it does I have found no other solution than to abandon parcel-making and resort to the Gunseli system of layering together the spinach mixture and filo. Use a rectangular oven dish and start with a layer of spinach and then a (possibly somewhat patchwork) layer of filo. Each layer of filo can be 2-3 sheets thick with butter/oil painted between the sheets. Repeat a few times. End with filo brushed with butter/olive oil.

8. Hopefully this won't happen to you. The technique of painting single sheets of filo with melted butter, folding, painting again, stuffing and folding several more times is best demonstrated in a diagram if no one is around to show you. Good luck!

9. When you have got all the borek triangles lined up on an oiled/lined baking tray (but not touching), give them a final painting with butter or olive oil.

10. Cook at 180°C (350°F, gas mark 4) for 30-60 minutes. Check after 20 minutes. Re-adjust position if some are browning more quickly than others. When they are ready, they'll be golden brown and the filo nicely crisped up.

TANGY TURTLE BEANS

This tasty bean stew was introduced to us by Inge Page—as well as being our Programme Coordinator, she is one of the college's great bean connoisseurs. In this recipe, black turtle beans are infused with whole orange halves giving them the uniquely piquant tang of citrus so often associated with Brazilian recipes. If you can get hold of organic oranges, so much the better. Their rind, unsprayed, will be far healthier. Serve with sour cream, green salad and either brown rice or cornbread.

For 4-6	For 35-40
1 large onion, chopped	11 large onions
2 cloves garlic, minced	22 cloves
1 red or green pepper, chopped	11
½ bulb fennel (or 1 stalk celery), chopped	6 bulbs (or 1 head)
8 oz (220 g/1¼ cups) black turtle beans	5½ lb (2.5 kg)
1 bay leaf	11 bay leaves
1 tsp ground cumin	3½-4 tbsp
1 tsp vinegar	3½-4 tbsp
2 tbsp tomato purée (paste)	6-8 fl oz (200 ml/¾-1 cup)
1 orange, washed and halved (with skin)	9
2 tsp fresh coriander leaves (optional)	2 oz (55 g)
salt and pepper to taste	1-3 tbsp

1. Soak the beans (with kombu, if available) in about 3 times their depth of water overnight.

2. Rinse beans, cover with fresh water, bring to the boil and simmer for approx. 1 hour until getting tender. Drain off surplus liquid and keep aside in case you need to use more later. Add some stock powder/cubes to help keep beans firm. Alternatively, a little salt can be added at this stage.

3. Chop onions, peppers and fennel in narrow 1½" (3 cm) strips. Mince garlic. Sauté together in olive oil.

4. Add ground cumin and bay leaves. Then add beans, tomato purée, vinegar, orange halves, and extra stock if necessary. Simmer with lid ajar for about one hour. Stir often to prevent burning.

5. Remove oranges, squeezing them against the side of the pan to get out the juice (salad tongs can be useful for this). Alternatively, place them in a large sieve or colander with a bowl underneath. Poke them with a wooden spoon and return the juice to the stew.

6. Check and adjust seasoning. If using fresh coriander, rough chop and stir two-thirds into the stew at the end of the cooking time. Garnish with the rest.

PLAITING PUFF PASTRY

1. Place pre-rolled rectangle of puff pastry on clean surface. Put filling down middle third, allowing 2½" (6 cm) at either end. With a knife, cut lines inwards on either side of mixture. Make sure they are opposite each other and do not go right up to the filling. Cut the corners off to form semi-circles at top and bottom.

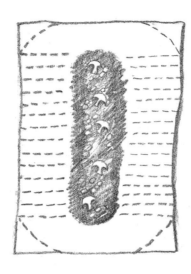

2. Gently fold the semi-circles of pastry at top and bottom over the mixture forming a 'hood' and a 'slipper'.

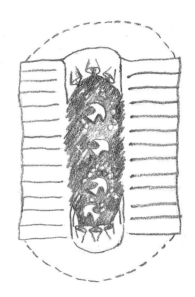

3. Fold the first left strip diagonally over the 'hood' and mixture at an angle towards your right. Next fold the first right-hand strip diagonally over the left one.

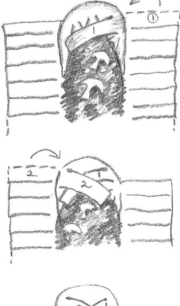

4. Repeat, always covering the ends of the previously folded strips with the next strip.

5. When you get to the bottom, tuck the ends of the last strips under the bottom of the pastry.

Carefully lift on to a prepared baking sheet, either with hands, or if the plait is long, using three flat spatulas—one under each end and one in the middle (three hands will also be necessary!).

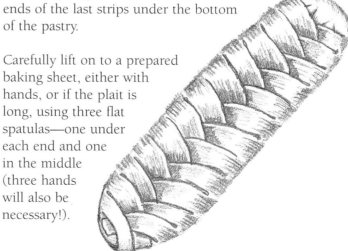

SPINACH & MUSHROOM PLAIT

When Debbie Hirsh first came to Schumacher College on Wolfgang Sachs' Ecological Economics course, she offered to cook Sunday supper for everyone. We knew she was a trained gourmet chef, and our expectations were high: we were not disappointed. That evening the most spectacular braided pastries emerged from the oven, all golden-brown and wanting to melt in our mouths. Nobody could imagine how she made them and they looked far too complicated to recreate.

Part of the secret was to cheat and use frozen puff pastry. Though it might have seemed against the whole-food principles of our cooking, this mass-produced pastry had only one E number and otherwise contained natural, all-vegan ingredients. Its performance was so satisfying, with none of the trouble of folding and chilling puff pastry, that we were soon using it to revitalize our lunches with a simplified version of Debbie's plait filled with spinach, mushroom and cheese.

Luckily, Debbie returned to the College and let us into the rest of the secret—how to plait pastry over the filling. It is surprisingly easy to learn and will transform your dining room into a French restaurant! The technical term for this plait is 'D'ortoise'. The filling can be varied to taste, using other vegetables, lentils, etc.—the key is to let the mixture cool and make sure it isn't too runny. For a vegan version, try using crumbled tofu instead of the cheese. If the small quantity seems too much for your family—even over a bank-holiday weekend—you can freeze one plait and bring it out later.

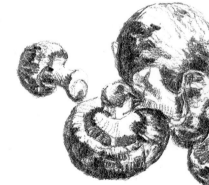

For 10-15 (1-2 pastries)	For 35-40 (5-6 pastries)
1 lb 10 oz (750 g) defrosted puff pastry	6½ lb (3 kg)
2 lb (900 g) frozen or fresh spinach	8 lb (3.6 kg)
12 oz (340 g/2 cups) chopped onions	3 lb (1.4 kg)
12 oz (340 g/3 cups) cheddar cheese, grated	3 lb (1.4 kg)
1¼ lb (560 g/7 cups) chopped mushrooms	5 lb (2.2 kg)
1 tbsp Dijon mustard	2-4 tbsp
pinch salt to taste	3-4 tsp
pinch freshly ground black pepper to taste	1-3 tsp

1. The night before you want to cook, remove the frozen pastry from the freezer to defrost. Also remove the spinach, if you are using the frozen variety. Leave at room temperature on a tray that will catch the drips.

2. Slice up the onions and sauté. Slice up the mushrooms and add them to the onions. Continue cooking until both are fairly well cooked.

3. If using fresh spinach, rinse, sort and chop roughly. Most of the stalk can be used, but discard dried or fibrous end parts. Steam spinach until wilted, and strain off surplus liquid. The spinach doesn't have to be well-

cooked. Frozen spinach doesn't require any pre-cooking. Tip it into a colander and strain off surplus liquid, pressing spinach against the walls of the colander with a wooden spoon—or your (clean) hands.

4. Combine the spinach with the mushrooms and onions and allow to cool.

5. Stir the grated cheese, pepper, salt and mustard into the spinach mixture. Taste and adjust seasoning.

6. Cut the pastry in quarters or thirds. Lightly flour a table top and begin rolling out the pastry with a floured rolling pin. Try and make the pastry a nice even rectangle, about 16" x 12" (40 x 30 cm). Moving it round and rolling it in the other direction can help. With experience, you'll find your own technique. Roll out all the pieces of pastry, making them only a few millimetres (say 1/8") thick. Pile them up on top of each other for convenience, if making the larger quantity.

7. Spoon some of the spinach mixture down the middle of the piece of pastry, leaving about 4" (10 cm) of pastry free at each side, and 3" (8 cm) on top and bottom (see diagram).

8. Braiding. Cut the pastry in parallel 1/2" (15mm) strips on either side of the filling, leaving about 3/8" (1 cm) between the edge of the filling and the end of the incision. Tuck the top and bottom edges over the top and bottom of the filling, so that the first strip hugs the filling. Now begin plaiting, diagonally laying one strip over the other, much as if you were making a 'French plait' on a girl's head. Hairdressers should have no problem with this! The square ends of the strips should end up tucked in and not showing. Tuck the last strips under the end of the pastry. The diagram should help.

9. If it all seems too much of a fuss, simply wrap the pastry around the mixture, making sure there is a good overlap. Try and keep the join underneath when you move it onto the baking tray. Press together the ends. Make a few diagonal cuts on the top, to allow air to escape.

10. Using two or three flat metal spatulas (and preferably two or three people) move the uncooked pastry plait on to the baking tray, which should be placed alongside it, to reduce the distance this rather wobbly thing has to travel.

11. Brush with beaten egg and, if you like, sprinkle with sesame seeds.

12. Bake at 180°C (350°F, gas mark 4) for about 1 hour or until golden brown. Check every now and then and turn around so that it cooks evenly. Once out of the oven, you may wish to transfer the pastry on to chopping boards for serving, again using three spatulas and four hands.

WALNUT & MUSHROOM BOLOGNESE

This combination of mushrooms, aubergines, tomato and walnuts creates a purple-brown sauce with a real substance to it. A garnish of freshly chopped parsley, whole walnuts and mushroom slices adds a hint of elegance and brightness. Our favourite choices of pasta to serve with this sauce are tagliatelle, penne or fusilli. Accompany with freshly grated parmesan or cheddar, and a mixed green salad studded with the reds of tomatoes, peppers, radishes or carrots.

For 4-6	For 35-40
6 oz (170 g/1 heaped cup) onion, chopped fine	3 lb (1.4 kg)
2 cloves garlic, sliced	15 cloves
½ tsp each ground cinnamon, allspice & ginger	1½ tbsp each
3 oz (85 g/¾ cup) walnuts, lightly toasted	1½ lb (500 g)
12 oz (300 g/4 cups) mushrooms, sliced	6 lb (2.7 kg)
12 oz (300 g/1½ cups) chopped tomatoes (fresh or canned)	6½ lb (3 kg)
1-2 tbsp tomato purée (paste)	8 fl oz (250 ml/1 cup)
1-2 tbsp soy sauce	6 fl oz (150 ml/¾ cup)
6 oz (160 g/1⅓ cups) aubergine, cubed & salted	3 lb (1.4 kg)
4-5 fl oz (150 ml/½ cup) red wine	1 bottle
5 fl oz (150 ml/⅔ cup) vegetable stock to thin	1-2 pints (½-1 litre/3-5 cups)
1-2 tsp oregano	3-5 tbsp
2 fl oz (50 ml/¼ cup) cream (optional)	1¼ pint (700 ml/3 cups)
1 lb 2 oz (500 g) pasta approx.	6½-7½ lb (3-3.4 kg)

1. Warm the oven to 180°C (350°F, gas mark 4) and toast the walnuts on a baking tray for 5-10 minutes. It is very easy to forget them, so use a timer. They should be just beginning to turn a caramel colour when ready; if they go dark brown they will be too bitter. Meanwhile, slice aubergine into small cubes and sprinkle with salt. Leave to stand for about 30 minutes to draw out any bitter juices. Drain well.

2. Sauté onion, garlic and spices until onions begin to go pearly. Add aubergines to onions and cook for a further few minutes. Keep a few of the best mushroom slices for garnishing, then add rest to the sauté, and continue to cook for a further 5 minutes. Add remaining ingredients. Cover and simmer for 30 minutes, stirring occasionally.

3. Begin preparing the pasta about 20 minutes before serving time. Allow 3-4 oz (85-110 g) per person.

4. Blending. Remove about half the mixture and blend it, fairly roughly, with a rod blender, or food processor. Recombine with the rest. (Alternatively blend all—or none!)

5. Add stock (or hot water) to achieve required consistency. Add cream (to taste) at end. Season to taste, and garnish with parsley, a few walnut halves and the reserved slices of elegantly cut raw mushroom.

SOLOMON'S STEW

This smoky three-bean stew evokes Mediterranean country cooking at its most romantic. Imagine that the cold winter evenings are creeping up; there are still a few red peppers on the bushes and a few more preserved in olive oil on the shelves, alongside jars of dried beans of all colours. Strands of dried tomatoes, onions and herbs dangle over the hob. There is still enough warmth in the manure heap to generate a few mushrooms. And, as the farmer has been converted to Buddhism by a passing Japanese tourist, he has learned to use tofu instead of bacon. When the family sit down to enjoy a warming bean stew around the fire that flickers in their inglenook, a family friend joins them for supper: Solomon the liberated pig!

For 10-15	For 40
8 oz (225 g/1¼ cups) chick peas	1½ lb (700 g)
8 oz (225 g/1¼ cups) butter beans	1½ lb (700 g)
8 oz (225 g/1¼ cups) red kidney beans	1½ lb (700 g)
½-1 pint (300-600 ml/1-2 cups) bean water	2-3 pints (1-2 litres/1-2 US quarts)
1 lb (450 g/3 cups) roughly chopped onions	3 lb (1.4 kg)
4-5 cloves finely sliced garlic	2-3 tbsp
1¼ lb (600 g/8 cups) halved open mushrooms	3½ lb (1.6 kg)
1¼ lb (600 g/3-4 medium-sized) red peppers, 1" squares	4 lb (1.8 kg)
2 bulbs fennel (or 4 stalks celery)	6 bulbs (or 1 head)
8 oz (225 g/1 cup) chopped fresh tomatoes	1½ lb (700 g)
2 lb (900 g) smoked tofu	6 lb (2.7 kg)
2 fl oz (55 ml/¼ cup) tamari to marinate tofu	6 fl oz (160 ml)
6-7 fl oz (200 ml/¾-1 cup) tomato purée (paste)	15-20 fl oz (4-600 ml)
5-6 tbsp chopped fresh parsley	3 oz (85 g/1¼ cups)
1-2 tbsp dried herbes de Provence	3-6 tbsp
pinch of salt and pepper to taste	1-2 tbsp salt, 1 tsp pepper
approx. 2 tsp vegetable stock powder to taste	2 tbsp
1 tbsp Dijon or pommery mustard	3 tbsp
a few tsps malt extract/honey/brown sugar to taste	3-6 tbsp

1. Soak beans overnight in three times their depth of cold water. Keep the different kinds of bean separate.

2. Cook the beans with bay leaves, still keeping each kind separate. This will take 50 minutes to 1½ hours—some beans take longer than others. You want them soft but still holding their shape.

3. Sauté the onions, garlic, red peppers, fennel (or celery) and herbes de Provence in olive oil in the bottom of a large casserole/saucepan.

4. After 15-20 minutes or so, add the mushrooms and continue to sauté for several minutes. Lastly add the fresh tomatoes and cook until all vegetables are tender.

5. Add the beans and enough of the bean water to almost cover the other ingredients: the beans will be peeping out above the liquid like frogspawn, and a generous saucy liquid will be bubbling all around them. Add tomato purée, salt, pepper and bouillon to taste. Also add malt extract, honey or brown sugar if you like. Continue cooking on a low heat.

6. Meanwhile, slice the smoked tofu width-wise into thinnish rectangles, about $3/16$" ($1/2$ cm) thick. Halve these in order to obtain rectangles of about $1 1/2$" (4 cm) in length. Toss these in tamari (or soya), then fry lightly in sunflower oil until they are fairly crispy and golden brown on both sides. Cover a plate with kitchen paper and carefully fish out the tofu pieces. Place them on the paper to absorb excess oil. (I sometimes omit the frying step to reduce the oil content of the stew and save time. In this case, you will need to handle the tofu with even greater care and minimize stirring.)

7. Carefully stir the tofu pieces into the stew and cook for a further 10-20 minutes. For smaller quantities, this further cooking can be done in a moderate oven, using a lid to prevent drying out. Oven cooking reduces the need to stir and helps to keep the tofu intact.

8. When everything is well cooked, richly seasoned, and ready to serve, stir two-thirds of the parsley into the stew. Garnish the top with the rest.

9. Accompaniments: cornbread, baked potatoes and brown rice all go well with this stew. You may also like to put out grated cheese or sour cream—just to complete the protein festival!

Woodcut by Peter Fox

HILARY'S RED RED RED CHILLI

What makes this chilli so red is the combination of red kidney beans, red bell peppers and red tomatoes. But what does RED taste like? Quite possibly, it tastes as earthy as well-cooked beans—and as fiery as chilli. The addition of a little honey brings heaven to earth and calms the fireworks. This bean stew goes well with either cornbread, brown rice or polenta. It can also be accompanied with a little grated cheese, sour cream, and a fresh green salad. Enjoy Hilary Nicholson's chilli and you will find yourself warmed through and spiced-up!

For 6-8	For 40 plus
12 oz (350 g/2 cups) red kidney beans	4½ lb (2.1 kg)
3 medium onions	3 lb (1.4 kg)
4 sticks celery	3 lb (1.4 kg/about 2 heads)
3 cloves garlic (or more)	10-20
1 red pepper	6
1 tbsp each coriander & cumin seed, ground	3 fl oz (100 ml/⅓ cup) of each
1-4 fresh red chillies (to taste)	2-6 (to taste)
1½ lb (700 g/3 cups) chopped tomatoes (fresh or tinned)	9 lb (4.1 kg)
6 tbsp tomato purée (paste)	18 fl oz (500 ml/2 cups)
1 tbsp paprika	4-6 tbsp
2-4 tbsp honey, to taste	6-12 fl oz (150-350 ml)
1 tbsp each oregano & herbes de Provence	6 tbsp each approx.
½-1 tsp salt, to taste	1-3 tbsp

1. Soak the red kidney beans overnight in 2 times their depth of water.

2. Next day, bring beans to the boil in fresh water with a sprig of bay leaf. When boiling, turn down and simmer with lid ajar for 1-1½ hours until just cooked. Avoid overcooking, as beans may go mushy or start splitting in half. Taste one to test, and switch off the burner when they are just ready.

3. Finely slice the onions and celery. Press the garlic. Slice the peppers in 1-1½" (2-4 cm) strips. Rough chop the tomatoes (small chunks) if using fresh. Then begin to fry the onions in the bottom of a saucepan large enough to hold the whole stew. After a few minutes add the celery, and then the red pepper, coriander and cumin.

4. Continue to cook all three ingredients together for a few minutes and then add the crushed garlic, very finely chopped chillies and herbs. Continue to cook until the onions are soft and the peppers and celery tender. Add honey, chopped tomatoes and purée.

5. Drain the beans (reserving some of the liquid in case you need to dilute the stew). Add them to tomato mixture. Add salt and paprika to taste. Continue to simmer for a while. Adjust seasoning as necessary.

HERBY SCALLOPED POTATOES WITH SMOKED CHEESE

When Fritjof Capra first came to Schumacher College in 1992, he was accompanied by his six-year-old daughter Juliette. In the two weeks before her mother (Elizabeth) arrived, the two consoled themselves with platefuls of scalloped potatoes, frequently raiding the huge walk-in fridge for more. I don't know if there is anything particularly Austrian (or American) about the combination of potatoes, cheese and cream, but it certainly comes into that universal category of 'comfort food', and will help to welcome a good night's sleep, even when an important member of your family is away.

If smoked cheese is not available, substitute with mature cheddar. The scalloped effect is made when the last overlapping layer of potatoes is arranged. This can make the whole thing quite decorative, good for special occasions as well as at the end of a long day. We usually serve scalloped potatoes with a fresh, mainly green salad, but a watery cooked vegetable such as red cabbage, steamed spring greens, baked tomatoes, marrow or courgette would also go well. As for dessert, it is really quite unnecessary to offer more than fresh fruit—though I suspect that in the ultimate Capra banquet, classic French apple tart would follow. But that's another story!

For 4-6	For 30-40
3 lb (1.4 kg) potatoes, parboiled & sliced	18 lb (8 kg)
8 oz (225 g/1½ cups) onions/leeks, chopped	6 lb (2.7 kg)
1-2 tsp dried Provençal or mixed herbs	3-4 tbsp
4 tbsp fresh parsley, marjoram etc., chopped	3½ oz (100 g/1½ cups)
8 oz (225 g/2 cups) cheddar, grated	3 lb (1.3 kg)
5 oz (140 g/1¼ cups) smoked cheese, grated	2 lb (900 g)
10 fl oz (300 ml/1¼ cups) milk	3 pints (1.7 litres/1¾ US quarts)
6 fl oz (160 ml/¾ cup) cream	2 pints (1.2 litres/5 cups)
and 2 tbsp flour	and 4 oz flour (160 ml/¾ cup)
4 oz (110 g/1 cup) dried brown breadcrumbs	1¼ lb (700 g/5 cups approx.)
3 tbsp butter, melted	10 oz (300 g/2½ sticks)

1. Scrub the potatoes and dig out any bad bits. If they are organic, there is no need to peel them.

2. Cover with cold water and bring to the boil. Simmer until a knife will just slide through the potatoes: they should be almost cooked, still quite firm and preferably not flaky. Allow 20-30 minutes, depending on quantity. Drain and leave to cool.

3. Meanwhile, sauté the onions and/or leeks lightly in some olive oil with the dried herbs. When they are beginning

to go transparent, they should be cooked enough—they don't need to be very soft as they will cook more in the oven.

4. Cut potatoes into thick slices of approx. ¼" (½ cm). Place a single layer of potatoes in the bottom of an ovenproof baking dish (or dishes). Scatter with half of the onions/leeks and fresh herbs, a sprinkling of salt and freshly ground black pepper, and half the grated cheeses. Place a new layer of potato slices and repeat, using up all the onions/leeks and cheese. Finish with a decorative layer of potatoes, overlapping them like roofing tiles.

5. Heat the milk and pour over the potatoes. (Using boiling milk makes a considerable difference to the cooking time when you are making the larger size portion). Whisk together the cream and flour and pour this over as well.

6. Scatter the breadcrumbs over the top, and, finally, drizzle with the melted butter.

7. Bake at 180°C (350°C, gas mark 4), uncovered, for 40-60 minutes, until brown and sizzling. When ready, the cheese should all have melted and fused with the piping hot potatoes. However, stick a knife in to check everything is heated through and the potatoes soft.

NO FRILLS MACARONI CHEESE

This must be the best-known comfort food we have. It's loaded with dairy, and whilst it may have had its origin in Italy, it is now part of every English child's upbringing. At the College we often serve macaroni cheese with green salad and homemade tomato chutney; at other times we serve it with a seasonal vegetable such as leeks, spring greens, marrow or baked tomatoes (nothing too heavy). Ideal when returning from a blustery outing to the sea or Dartmoor with red cheeks, a cold nose and a good appetite!

For 4-6	For 35-40
2 oz (55 g/½ stick) butter	1 lb (450 g)
5 tbsp flour	12½ oz (350 g/2½ cups)
1 pint (600 ml/2½ cups) milk	8 pints (4.6 litres/4¾ US quarts)
2 tsp Dijon mustard	3 fl oz (75 ml/⅓ cup)
6 oz (170 g/1½ cups) grated cheddar cheese	3 lb (1.4 kg)
pinch salt and pepper to taste	1-3 tsp salt, 1 tsp pepper
8 oz (220 g/3 cups) macaroni	4 lb (1.8 kg)
4 oz (110 g/¾ cup) dried breadcrumbs approx.	1 lb (450 g/4 cups approx.)

1. Melt the butter on a gentle heat, making sure it doesn't burn. Add the flour and cook gently for a couple of minutes, stirring continuously.

2. Meanwhile heat the milk to almost boiling (it will be beginning to steam). This is especially important when making large quantities. If you don't pre-heat the milk, it will take a very long time to bring the sauce to the temperature where it will begin to thicken and the chance of burning is much higher.

3. Now add the steaming milk to the roux of flour and butter, stirring constantly. Bring to the boil, then reduce the heat and simmer for a few minutes, stirring frequently. The sauce should now have thickened, so add 80% of the cheese (remember to reserve some for the topping) and stir until it has all melted. Season to taste and turn off the heat. Put a lid on to keep the heat in.

4. Cook the pasta in boiling salted/oiled water for 10 minutes or so (see instructions on packet). Drain well. Mix macaroni and sauce and pour into oven dish/es that are about 2-3" (6-7 cm) deep, until almost full. Alternatively, put the pasta into dishes first, then pour the cheese sauce over the top and stir.

5. Sprinkle top with fine brown breadcrumbs, grated cheese and a few dabs of butter.

6. Bake at 180°C (350°F, gas mark 4) for 40-60 minutes, or until golden brown and crispy on top.

7. Vegan variation: instead of cheese sauce, use a sauce made with nutritional yeast flakes, which have a pleasantly nutty flavour. You could use the sherry sauce recipe, though you may wish to leave out the sherry.

RATATOUILLE – LASAGNE

In this recipe for lasagne, two distinct concoctions are layered into one rich, tomatoey pasta dish. The perfect complement to the smell of tomato is that of melted cheese, bubbling and golden on the top of the lasagne as it emerges from the oven. And, in case one complement isn't enough, try serving up the lasagne with lashings of crispy garlic-sodden bread, as well as a fresh green salad.

Because ratatouille stands as a dish in its own right, and as it seems to improve with a day's keeping, you may like to make extra amounts of this delicious Mediterranean ensemble of aubergines, peppers, courgettes and tomatoes. It can be served hot or cold with rice, pasta, baked potatoes or bread.

A. For the Ratatouille

For 4-6	For 30	For 60
4 tbsp olive oil approx.	15 fl oz (400 ml/2 cups)	30 fl oz (800 ml/3¾ cups)
4 oz (110 g/²/₃ cup) onion, chopped	2 lb (900 g)	4 lb (1.8 kg)
2 cloves garlic	6-10	12-20
8 oz (220 g) aubergines (1 small/medium)	4 lb (1.8 kg)	8 lb (3.6 kg)
8 oz (220 g) courgettes (one 8"-long)	4 lb (1.8 kg)	8 lb (3.6 kg)
1 red pepper	8	16
8 oz (220 g/1 cup) tomatoes, chopped (canned/fresh)	4 lb (1.8 kg)	8 lb (3.6 kg)
2 tbsp tomato purée (paste)	8 fl oz (200 ml/1 cup)	16 fl oz (450 ml/2 cups)
¹/₂ tsp each dried basil & oregano	1 tbsp of each	2 tbsp of each
2 tbsp each fresh parsley, basil & oregano	5 fl oz (150 ml) of each	10 fl oz (300 ml/1¹/₄ cups) of each
2 fl oz (50 ml/¹/₄ cup) red wine, to taste (or use medium sherry)	10-15 fl oz (300-400 ml/1-2 cups)	15-20 fl oz (400-500 ml/2-3 cups)

1. Quarter the aubergines lengthways and then slice into ½" (1 cm) thick segments. Sprinkle with salt and leave for 30 mins to sweat out the bitterness. Rinse, drain and pat dry.

2. Prepare the other vegetables, cutting them all to roughly the same size but keeping in separate piles.

3. The ratatouille can be made either by sautéeing the vegetables on the top of the stove, or by roasting them inside the oven. I find that for the larger quantities it is easier to roast the peppers, courgettes and aubergines. This avoids having to stand and stir huge quantities of vegetables that may otherwise burn, and the taste is very good. Place the vegetables in separate baking trays, massage with olive oil and roast at 200°C (400°F, gas mark 6) stirring occasionally until tender. Then combine with the sautéed onions and garlic, chopped tomatoes, red wine, salt and pepper and dried herbs and cook for another 30-40 minutes.

4. Whilst the other vegetables are in the oven, the onions and garlic can be sautéed until opalescent; the fresh herbs can be chopped and the tomatoes (if fresh) can be sliced. If fresh herbs are not available, double the quantity of the more intense dried herbs and add at the earlier stage. If tomatoes are not in season, the canned variety will probably prove more flavoursome—as well as cheaper.

5. If sautéeing the ratatouille, add the courgette and pepper to the onion and cook for a further 10-15 minutes. Sauté the aubergine separately in oil until soft. Add aubergine, tomatoes, purée, wine and dried herbs to the onions (shift to a saucepan if necessary). Cover and simmer for 30 minutes or until tender. Season and stir in the fresh herbs.

6. Additional seasoning. A spoonful or three of brown sugar, honey or malt extract will help to remove any sharpness. Adding a little coarse-grain or Dijon mustard can also be nice. Leave for a few hours or overnight to allow flavours to mature. Accompany with grated cheese if serving hot.

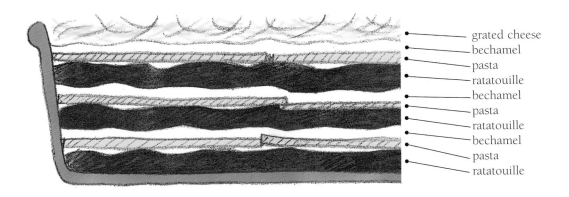

grated cheese
bechamel
pasta
ratatouille
bechamel
pasta
ratatouille
bechamel
pasta
ratatouille

B. Bechamel Sauce

For 1¼ pints (700 ml/3 cups)	For 5 pints (2.8 litres/3 US quarts)
2 oz (55 g/½ stick) butter	8 oz (220 g/2 sticks) butter
5 tbsp flour	6½ oz (180 g/1⅓ cups)
1¼ pints (700 ml/3 cups) milk	5 pints (2.8 litres/3 US quarts)
1-2 pinches salt	1 tbsp approx.
1 pinch pepper	1-2 tsp
1 pinch grated nutmeg	½-1 tsp

1. Heat the milk in a saucepan until it begins to simmer. This pre-heating of the milk is especially important when making the larger quantities, to avoid burning. Meanwhile gently melt the butter in another saucepan (this should be plenty large enough to hold the volume of milk required). Add the flour to the melted butter and stir continuously for 2 minutes (this is called making a roux). Be careful not to let the mixture brown.

2. Add the almost boiling milk to the roux and stir briskly and continuously with a whisk or wooden spoon. Keep scraping the bottom of the pan all over to prevent burning. Bring back to the boil and cook for 5-20 minutes, until custard-thick. Stir regularly. Season in accordance with your recipe.

3. Troubleshooting: if in a moment of negligence the sauce does burn, avoid scraping a burned area on the bottom of a pan with your spoon as it will quickly contaminate the taste of the rest of the sauce with a bitter edge that is not easily diluted. Immediately transfer the sauce into a new pan. If the sauce gets lumpy, the situation can be retrieved by blending it, preferably using a hand-held rod blender.

C. Assembling the Lasagne

For 10	For 35-40
Ratatouille for 4-6	for 30
1¼ pints (700 ml/3 cups) bechamel sauce	5 pints (2.8 litres/3 US quarts)
6 oz (175 g/1½ cups) grated cheddar	1½ lb (700 g)
8 oz (225 g/2 cups) grated smoked cheddar	2 lb (900 g)
2 oz (55 g/1 cup) grated whole parmesan	8 oz (225 g/4 cups)
10-16 oz (275-500 g) no-pre-cook lasagne verde	3-4 lb (1.3-1.8 kg)

1. Stir the parmesan and about half the cheddar and three-quarters of the smoked cheese into the hot bechamel sauce (if using the drier, pre-grated variety of parmesan, use only ½ cup/2 cups). Finish off the seasoning, tasting to see how much salt and pepper are needed.

2. You should now have all the elements at your fingertips—ratatouille, bechamel sauce, no-pre-cook lasagne tiles—and a little pile of grated cheese for the top. You will also need 1-6 large rectangular or square ovenproof

casseroles 2-3" (6-7 cm) deep. In the College kitchen we use two large stainless steel casseroles measuring 19 x 10" to make enough lasagne for 40.

3. Begin to assemble the lasagne by spreading a layer of ratatouille over the bottom of the casseroles. It should be a bumpy $1/2$" ($1\frac{1}{2}$ cm) thick (see diagram). Next a layer of pasta, laying it out as if you were making a patio, covering all the ratatouille. Where necessary, break off corners of pasta to give a snug fit. (If using traditional pre-cook lasagne, boil it first according to the instructions on the package.)

4. Now spread a generous layer of bechamel sauce over the pasta, about $1/4$" ($1/2$ cm) thick. Then go back to the ratatouille and spread another layer of this. Repeat the three layers until all the white sauce is used up. Finish with a layer of bechamel—and then top this with the remaining grated cheese. Usually, this mixture will make a three-pasta layered lasagne, although this rather depends on how thick you make the layers in between (which is why it is difficult to estimate how much pasta will be needed).

5. Bake at 180°C (350°F, gas mark 4) for 40-60 minutes until golden brown and delicious on top. By this time the pasta should have absorbed moisture from the sauces and cooked through—poke with a knife and peer in if you want to check. The sauces will also probably be bubbling up around the edges.

6. Variations: for a vegan version, the bechamel sauce can be made with soya milk and margarine. The cheese should be omitted. A handful of cashews can be added to the ratatouille for extra protein if you like, and the top can be decorated with pumpkin seeds on top of the white sauce. For wheat-free diets, a half-quantity of cornflour or arrowroot can be used, and special gluten-free lasagne purchased. For spinach and mushroom lasagne, substitute the ratatouille with the mixture prepared for the plait on page 71, minus the cheese.

PENNE WITH PESTO, RED PEPPER & MUSHROOMS

Fresh basil has a uniquely sweet and strong aroma. It is considered sacred in India, where it is known as *tulsi*. Any visiting Martians landing at Schumacher College during the basil harvest might well take it to be our sacred leaf too, for as the summer season draws to a close, the Dartington market garden begins to uproot its annual basil plants and aromatic sackloads of the precious herb arrive—sometimes unexpectedly—at the kitchen door. Participants, volunteers and staff found sitting comfortably anywhere in the dining room must beware, for they will immediately have their hands enlisted in the process of detaching leaf from stem. All this so that the basil can be whizzed up with olive oil and preserved while fresh for the delectation of future participants. Perhaps the most delicious use of basil is to make it into pesto genovese by adding (alongside the olive oil) garlic, parmesan and either pine nuts or cashews.

One of our favourite—and simplest—welcoming suppers consists of penne (a tubular pasta with slanting ends) coated in pesto. To this we add generous nuggets of roast red pepper and mushroom, tossing them in like coins into a wishing well. The proportions of the ingredients traditionally used in pesto making would have varied with individual tastes and availability, so this recipe is just a guideline. I normally allow 3-4 oz (85 g) dry pasta per person when serving it as a main course.

For about 8	For 30-35
For the Pesto	
6 fl oz (170 ml/³/₄ cup) olive oil	24 fl oz (650 ml/3 cups)
8 oz (225 g/4 cups) fresh basil leaves	2 lb (900 g)
2¹/₂ oz (60g/1¹/₄ cups) whole parmesan, grated	10 oz (275 g/5 cups)
4 oz (110 g/1 cup) pine nuts/cashew pieces	1 lb (450 g/4 cups)
3-5 cloves garlic	15-20
2-3 tsp lemon juice (optional)	juice from 1 lemon
1-2 pinches salt	1-2 tsp
pinch freshly ground black pepper	¹/₂-1 tsp
1 lb 2 oz (500 g) open mushrooms	4 lb 8 oz (2 kg)
4-5 good size red peppers	15-20
1¹/₂ lb (700 g) pasta	6 lb (2.8 kg)

Pesto

1. Pick over the basil, discarding black leaves, tough stems etc. (the finer, tender stalks are usually OK, but try biting one if you are unsure). Wash lightly in cold water and spin or pat dry. Blend basil and oil in food processor using the knife attachment. (If you are freezing the pesto, do so now, attaching a note to say what quantity of parmesan/nuts should be added in the future).

2. Spread the pine nuts or cashews on a baking tray and roast in a moderate oven for 5-10 minutes until just lightly browning on the edges. Cool. With regard to special diets, it may be useful to remember that people with nut allergies will often be able to eat pine nuts, but not cashews. Check, if relevant.

3. Add nuts, garlic cloves and blend again. (Remove any pesto required for vegan diets at this stage. Additional nuts can be blended into the vegan pesto if you like.) Add the grated parmesan cheese. If you can afford to buy whole parmesan and grate it yourself you will find the flavour much better. Otherwise stick with the almost sand-like, pre-grated parmesan. Add salt and pepper. Blend again. Add more oil if necessary, or lemon juice.

Red pepper and mushroom

4. Slice the red peppers into generous strips that will readily intermingle with the penne (and not all fall to the bottom). Place on a baking tray, one layer thick. Massage generously with olive oil and roast in the oven for 30-40 minutes, until cooked and beginning to brown at the edges. The mushrooms can, likewise, be cut in thick slices, halved or quartered and roast in the oven with olive oil for 20-30 minutes. Some people prefer to sauté them in a frying pan.

5. Keep the red peppers and mushrooms warm until you are ready to serve. However do not let them linger too long in a hot oven or they will shrivel up. Turn down the temperature—or re-heat just before serving time.

6. Prepare the pasta about 15 minutes before serving time. Allow 25 minutes if you are making the larger quantity, as it will take longer for the pasta to cook and to put the dish together. Have the water boiling in advance of this. Add a pinch of salt and a dash of oil to the water and stir the pasta to the boil. Once boiling turn the temperature down to a simmer and cook for the time recommended on the pasta packet (8-12 minutes). Test. Some people say pasta is ready when you can throw it at a wall and it sticks! Strain in a colander and immediately add the pesto to stop the pasta sticking to itself.

7. Stir the pesto carefully into the strained pasta using a wooden spoon. Tip the coated pasta into the dish you are going to serve it in, tossing in the peppers and mushrooms as you go. If it is easier, layers of penne can be followed by (scattered) layers of roast vegetable. The main thing is to avoid simply mixing everything together in one go, as the bright colours of the roast peppers, etc., will be dulled by the pesto. Also you need to ensure you have plenty of peppers and mushrooms left for the top—a scattering of pine nuts or cashews can also add to the attraction!

8. Serve with a mixed green salad, or a tomato salad and a green salad. Additional grated parmesan may also be offered in a small bowl.

CHEESE, CASHEW & WALNUT ROAST

This delicious, succulent, nut roast has left many carnivores wondering why they bother! It is a favourite for our last night supper at the end of courses and an excellent substitute for turkey at Christmas or roast beef on Sunday. Serve it up with plenty of seasonal vegetables and lashings of rich sherry sauce.

Many thanks must go to Ed Brown and the Zen Centre for the leap of imagination that brought together brown rice, cheese, eggs, nuts and vegetables in a nut roast—and soya sauce and sherry in a gravy.

For 6+	For 35-40
6 oz (170 g/1 cup) onion, finely diced	2 lb (900 g)
6 oz (200 ml/2 cups) chopped mushrooms	2 lb (900 g)
2 cloves garlic, minced	8-12
1 medium red pepper, finely diced	5
2-3 sticks celery, finely diced	1 head
1 tsp each dried thyme, sage, marjoram	2 tbsp of each
9 oz (250 g/1½ cups) cooked brown rice (about 3½ oz/100 g/⅔ cup when uncooked)	2½ lb (1.1 kg) (1 lb/450 g/2⅔ cups)
4 oz (110 g/1 cup) walnuts, chopped fine	1¼ lb (600 g)
4 oz (110 g/1 cup) cashew pieces	1¼ lb (600 g)
5 medium eggs	20
6 oz (180 g/¾ cup) cottage cheese	2 lb (900 g)
12 oz (340 g/3 cups) grated cheese (including cheddar, smoked cheddar, Red Leicester)	3 lb 12 oz (1.7 kg)
4 tbsp/¼ cup chopped fresh herbs (incl. parsley, sage, rosemary & thyme)	3-4 oz (100 g/1½ cups)
1 tbsp Dijon mustard	4-5 tbsp
salt and pepper to taste	2-3 tsp
olive oil for sautéeing	a little more

1. Sauté onion and celery in olive oil until beginning to go transparent.

2. Add mushrooms, garlic, red pepper, dried herbs, salt and pepper. Cook until mixture is soft, stirring regularly to avoid burning.

3. Combine all ingredients in a large bowl and mix well.

4. Line a 2 lb (1 kg) loaf tin (seven tins for larger quantity) with baking parchment. The simplest way to do this is to use two pieces that will cross over on the base of the tin—a narrow one for length of tin and a wide one for

width. Fill to, at most, 3" (7 cm) deep. Fold over paper, to help prevent drying out. If the mixture is too deep, the outside may get rather leathery before the inside is properly set.

5. Bake at 180° C (350°F, gas mark 4) for about 1½ hours until firm. A knife inserted will come out wet but relatively clean showing that the eggs have set. Remove from the oven and allow to stand for 5-10 minutes before turning out and serving. Garnish with roughly chopped parsley. Carve into generous slices. Can also be served cold (pre-slice and arrange on a plate).

6. For a dairy-free version, omit the cheese, and also eggs if necessary. Instead, add crumbled tofu to the mixture: 9 oz (250 g) small quantity/3 lb (1.3 kg) large.

Sherry Sauce

A rich vegetarian gravy to accompany nut roast, rissoles, freshly cooked vegetables and roast potatoes.

For 6-8	For 35-40
makes 1½ pints (850 ml/3½ cups)	makes 7½ pints (4.2 litres/4½ US quarts)
1 pint (600 ml/2½ cups) stock	5 pints (3 litres/3 US quarts)
3 tbsp nutritional yeast flakes	1½ oz (40 g/1 cup)
4 tbsp (¼ cup) plain white flour	6 oz (170 g/1¼ cups)
1 tsp marjoram (dried)	2 tbsp
2 fl oz (75 ml/½ cup) organic sunflower oil	10 fl oz (300 ml)
¾ oz (20 g/1½ tbsp) butter	4 oz (110 g)
2 tbsp soy sauce	5 fl oz (150 ml)
1 tbsp Dijon mustard	3 fl oz (100 ml)
2 fl oz (55 ml/¼ cup) medium sherry*	10 fl oz (300 ml)
2 cloves crushed garlic	10 cloves
freshly ground black pepper to taste	freshly ground black pepper to taste

1. Place nutritional yeast flakes, dried marjoram and flour in a saucepan large enough to hold the volume of liquid in the recipe. Turn the heat on and stir these dry ingredients briefly with a wooden spoon until getting hot and beginning to give off a distinctive smell (somewhat nutty, somewhat toasty).

2. Add oil and butter and continue to cook, stirring regularly, for 2 minutes.

3. Whisk in stock and bring to the boil. Lower heat and simmer for 5 minutes. If stock is not available, add water and season with additional vegetable stock powder/cubes after you have added the soya sauce.

4. Add soy sauce, mustard, garlic, pepper and sherry. Cook for a further 2 minutes. Thin if necessary. Adjust seasoning to taste.

   *If sherry is not available, use a medium red wine and a spoon of sugar/honey to taste.

SAVOURY VEGETABLE CRUMBLE (PELICAN PIE)

This satisfying combination of vegetables and chestnuts, with a rich gravy and a crumbling, slightly cheesy topping, makes a great all-in-one family supper. It can be served with potatoes and green vegetables or a green salad. Vary the vegetables with the seasons, but always try to include many root vegetables which will keep their shape when cooked, such as carrots.

This recipe was first officially made by an enthusiastic group of 'pelicans' on a course exploring the use of ritual in our society today. Making 'Pelican Pie', like all good rituals, involves several stages, and a climax. This must be when you discover that the whole is greater than the sum of the parts . . . by eating it!

For 5-7 approx.	For 40 approx.
Crumble	
3 oz (85 g/1 cup) rolled/porridge oats	1 lb (450 g)
5 oz (140 g/1 cup) flour	1 lb 12 oz (800 g)
2 oz (60 g/1 cup) malted wheat flakes*	12 oz (340 g/6 cups)
2 oz (60 g/½ cup) chopped walnuts	12 oz (340 g/3 cups)
4 oz (110 g/1 stick) butter	1½ lb (700 g)
4 oz (110 g/1 cup) grated cheddar	1½ lb (700 g)
4 tsp parmesan (pre-grated is OK)	4 oz (110 g/1 cup)
1-2 tsp dried sage	2-3 tbsp
pinch each salt & freshly ground black pepper	1 tsp each
Filling	
6 oz (170 g/3 cups) mushrooms	2 lb (900 g)
4 oz (110 g/1 cup) leeks	1½ lb (700g)
12 oz (350 g/2½ cups) carrots	4 lb (1.8 kg)
8 oz (225 g/2¼ cups) onions	2½ lb (1.4 kg)
6 oz (170 g/1¼ cups) squash or parsnip	2 lb (900 g)
6 oz (170 g/1¼ cups) turnip or swede	2 lb (900 g)
2 medium sticks celery	1 head
5 oz (140 g/1 cup) dried chestnuts	1½ lb (700g)
1-3 tbsp freshly chopped parsley, sage, rosemary & thyme (half quantity if dried)	2-3 oz (55-85 g/1-1½ cups approx.)
15-20 fl oz (500-600 ml/2-2½ cups) sherry sauce	4-5 pints (2-2½ litres/2½-3 US quarts)

1. Soak dried chestnuts in cold water for several hours, or overnight. Then pick out any woody bits, and boil for 30-40 minutes until cooked.

Crumble Topping

2. Put the flour and oats in a bowl and slice in the butter. Once the butter has softened to room temperature, you can begin to lightly rub it in with your finger tips, until a rough, breadcrumb-like consistency is obtained. Don't press together into a lump. Then add the wheat flakes*, grated cheese, salt, pepper, herbs and parmesan. Mix loosely together.

Filling

3. The carrots, parsnips or squash, turnips or swedes, and leeks need to be prepared for par-boiling. Wash them and peel as necessary. If the leeks are not too earthy, cut them in ½" (1½ cm) rings, then wash again. Chop the other vegetables in similar nuggets, about ¾" (2 cm) wide. The root vegetables can be cooked together in salted boiling water until almost tender (but not too soft as they will cook a little more in the oven). They need to be acceptable to eat if, perchance, they don't cook any more! The leeks and squash will cook more quickly, so put them in a separate pan of boiling water, squash first. Again, cook until they are just ready. Reserve up to 5 pints (2.8 litres/3 US quarts) of the cooking water to make the sauce with.

4. Rough chop the celery and onions, and begin to sauté in olive oil. Halve or quarter the mushrooms (depending on how big they are), to achieve generous sized pieces. Add the mushrooms to the sauté and cook some more, until everything is just cooked. Finally, add the freshly chopped herbs and turn off the heat. If using dried herbs, use half the quantity and add at the same time as the mushrooms.

5. Make the sherry sauce (see separate recipe. If making the larger quantity, halve the recipe for 7½ pints, and make up to 4 pints, with extra water if necessary). Use the vegetable water as stock. Then mix together all the vegetables and chestnuts with the sherry sauce (dilute with a little extra vegetable water if the mixture seems too dry). You can do this in a large bowl or saucepan—or in the bottom of the baking dishes in which you are going to cook the crumble. Check seasoning and pat the vegetables down a little so they are spread out evenly in the dish, with enough space to hold the crumble. Sprinkle the crumble mixture lightly over the vegetables. Don't press it down as this can make it too solid. It should be about ¾" (1½ cm) thick.

6. Bake the 'Pelican Pie' in the oven for 40-60 minutes at 180 °C (350°F, gas mark 4). The crumble should be golden brown, turning a little more toffee-coloured at the edges. Stick knife in to check the vegetables are tender.

* wheat flakes are often sold as part of a muesli base, but use crumbled weetabix if you cannot get hold of them.

WENDY COOK'S POLENTA PIE

Wendy Cook arrived from Majorca to live with us at Schumacher College, bringing her own knife and her own apron. True to her name, she is a cook through and through—and has studied cooking in many different guises, from French Cordon Bleu to Japanese macrobiotic. But above all it is her intuitive sense of what is rich and delicious that inspires her cooking, and has nurtured all of us.

At the heart of Wendy's Mexican-Italian menu is her unique version of Polenta Pie. She normally serves this with a tomato sauce (that includes peppers, onion, celery, carrot and courgette), with a bean stew, with guacamole, with sour cream, with green salad—and finally, with lots of love.

As an alternative to the cooked tomato sauce, a fresh spicy salsa also complements the polenta nicely. If all these additions sound a bit daunting, just simplify matters and accompany the polenta with no more than a leafy salad. It's almost a banquet in itself!

For 8-10	For 35-40
1 lb (450 g/3 cups) coarse orangey-yellow polenta	3¼ lb (1½ kg)
2¼ pints (1.3 litres/5½ cups) water approx.	8 pints (4½ litres/4¾ US quarts)
6 eggs, separated	20
1 red pepper, finely diced	3
1 green pepper, finely diced	3
1 large onion, finely diced	3
3 cloves garlic, minced	9
1 tsp chopped sage	1 tbsp
12 oz (340 g/3 cups) cheddar, grated	2½ lb (1.1 kg)
2½ oz (60 g/¾-1 cup) parmesan, grated	8 oz (220 g/2-3 cups)
½ oz (10 g/2 tbsp) pine nuts (to sprinkle on top)	1-2 oz (40 g/¼-½ cup)
½ tsp salt approx.	2-4 tsp (to taste)
1-2 pinches pepper	1-2 tsp (to taste)
olive oil and butter for cooking	olive oil and butter for cooking

1. The first thing is to get the polenta cooking. Put a little olive oil and butter in the bottom of a fairly large, thick saucepan. With the heat on, stir in the polenta grain with a wooden spoon for a few minutes.

2. After a few minutes, add the water to the polenta. Bring to the boil, stirring regularly. Turn the heat down and let simmer while you get on with preparing the other ingredients. Stir regularly to avoid burning. It will need 15-20 minutes to thicken to porridginess. Leave to cool for 10 minutes.

3. Chop the peppers finely. Reserve some of these on a saucer for decoration later on. Sauté the rest in olive oil

with the diced onion, minced garlic and chopped sage.

4. Grate the cheddar cheese and, if necessary, the parmesan. Stir most of the cheese into the cooked polenta mixture. Stir the sautéed peppers into the polenta as well.

5. Oil 1/4 baking dishes. They will need to be 2-3" (6-7 cm) deep.

6. Separate the egg whites from the yolks, ready for whipping. Though it may help to get the eggs separated ahead of time, avoid whisking the egg whites until the polenta mixture has cooled a bit. Otherwise either the eggs may scramble or you may have to re-whip the whites. Once whipped to snowy peaks, fold the egg white carefully and minimally into the polenta. Be gentle—do not beat!

7. Pour into the oiled baking dishes. The mixture should be about $1^1/_2$-2" (3-4 cm) deep and have room to rise.

8. Finish off the top with a scattering of pine nuts, grated cheddar and the reserved chopped peppers, which can be tossed in a little olive oil to help them roast.

9. Bake for about 40-50 minutes (smaller quantity)/$1^1/_2$ hours (larger quantity) in a moderate oven (180°C, 350°F, gas mark 4). When cooked, the polenta should have puffed up quite a bit and become a glowing golden brown on top. The mixture will have set, so if you stick a knife in, it'll come out wet and covered with no more than a few grains.

SIJ'S SPICY STUFFED PEPPERS

Sij (alias Sarah Davis) first arrived on Victor Papanek's ecological architecture course as part of a round-the-world trip from South Africa. She was probably the first person to stuff a pepper at the college, and this recipe owes a lot to her. Traditionally, capsicum or bell peppers are stuffed with rice and sometimes mincemeat. In this version, however, they are stuffed with a very tasty—and completely vegan—concoction that includes crumbled tempeh and tofu alongside a medley of fruit and vegetables. The peppers are accompanied by two sauces: one warm, red and spicy; the other cool, nutty and a little creamy.

For 5-6	For 40-45
5-6 medium red, green and yellow peppers	40-45
4 oz (110 g) tofu, crumbled	1¼ lb (1 kg/4 packs)
7 oz (200 g) tempeh, crumbled	3¼ lb (1½ kg/6 packs)
5 oz (140 g/1 cup) onion, finely diced	2¼ lb (1 kg)
2-4 cloves garlic, crushed	12-16
2 medium red tomatoes, diced	15
1 medium apple, cored and finely chopped	8
1 medium courgette, diced	8
4 tbsp raisins	10 oz (275 g/2 cups)
4 tbsp almonds, oven roast and chopped	10 oz (275 g/2 cups)
½ tsp powdered cinnamon	1 tbsp
1 tsp ground cumin	2 tbsp
pinch cayenne pepper	1½ tsp
pinch salt (to taste)	1-2 tbsp (to taste)
tabasco (to taste)	to taste
8 fl oz (225 ml/1 cup) tomato juice	2½ pints (1½ litres/1½ US quarts)
a little fresh coriander leaf	1-2 oz (25-55 g/½ cup)
(for garnishing/hot sauce)	

1. Rinse the peppers and then slice in half lengthways through, or alongside, the stalk. Leave the stalk in place for structural and decorative reasons, but carefully scoop out the seeds using a small sharp knife to carve them away from the base of the stalk without damaging the bowl shape of the pepper. Also remove any large pieces of whiter flesh that may pose an obstacle to filling the pepper.

2. Place all the peppers cut side down on a sheet of baking parchment (or an oiled baking tray). Paint the outer skin with olive oil and cook at 180°C (350°F, gas mark 4) until beginning to sizzle and cook. They will have the opportunity to cook more later on, but since one of the major complaints with stuffed peppers is that the shells are still crunchy, it is good to get them half to three-quarters cooked in advance of stuffing. Alternatively, cook pepper halves briefly in boiling water—maybe not as tasty, but will reduce the oil content, if this is a concern.

3. Sauté the onions, garlic, courgette, cumin and cayenne pepper together until soft. Add the tomatoes, apples and raisins. Cover and simmer until apple is soft. Stir occasionally. Then toast the almonds in the oven for about 7-10 minutes at 180°C. Their skins should just be beginning to split down the centre. Chop roughly with a mezzaluna or in your food processor.

4. Add the crumbled tofu and tempeh, two-thirds of the almonds and the vinegar to the other mixture. Simmer for a further 5 minutes and season with salt. Reserve the remaining almonds on a saucer for garnishing later on.

5. Stuff the pepper halves and place in baking dishes. There should be enough of the mixture to build a little heap of it in each pepper. Start by making a fairly small heap, and then go back, adding a little more mixture, depending on how much you have left over once you have done the first round. Gently press the mixture into place with your (clean) hands, ensuring it is all sticking together and relatively smooth on top. Pour the tomato juice over the stuffed peppers so that it covers them and the bottom of the baking dish. Add a few shakes of tabasco to taste, if you like. Cover loosely with aluminium foil and bake at 180°C (350°F, gas mark 4) for 35-45 minutes.

6. Before serving, remove foil and scatter with the remaining chopped almonds and loosely chopped coriander, if available. Serve with brown rice, a green salad—and the following two sauces, which people can add to taste at the table.

Creamy Walnut Sauce

For 4-6	For 40
4 fl oz (110 ml/½ cup) yoghurt	32 fl oz (900 ml/4 cups)
2 oz (55 g/½ cup) toasted walnuts	1 lb (450 g/3 cups)
3 oz (85 g/6 tbsp) cream cheese	1½ lb (700 g)
2 fl oz (55 ml/¼ cup) milk	16 fl oz (450 ml/2 cups)
1 tsp ground cinnamon	3 tbsp
pinch cayenne to taste	2 tsp
pinch salt to taste	to taste

1. Spread the walnuts out on a baking tray and bake for 8-10 minutes at 180°C (350°F, gas mark 4) until beginning to sizzle. They should be just beginning to turn golden brown at the edges—but not toffee-brown or they will be too bitter. Cool.

2. Place all ingredients together in your blender and blend to a purée. Taste and adjust seasoning.

Hot Spicy Tomato Sauce

For 4-6	For 40
7 oz (200 g/³⁄₄ cup) canned tomatoes	3¹⁄₂ lb (1.6 kg)
¹⁄₂ green pepper, fine diced	4 small
4 tbsp onion, fine diced	12 oz (350 g/2 cups)
¹⁄₂ chilli (or to taste), diced	3-5
1-2 tsp fresh coriander leaves (if available)	4 tbsp
¹⁄₂ tsp ground coriander	1 tbsp
¹⁄₂ tsp ground cumin	1 tbsp
pinch salt to taste	¹⁄₂ tsp to taste

1. Prepare all ingredients. Place in blender/liquidizer and blend until smooth.

2. Simmer the sauce for about twenty minutes.

3. Adjust seasoning and serve hot.

SLOW PIZZA

Pizza must be one of the most delicious of all Italian inventions—and one of the country's best known exports. Originally it may have been devised as a way of using up left-over dough to create a sort of cooked open sandwich. Nowadays, however, the practice of breadmaking in the home has almost completely vanished, and if you make pizza from scratch, preparing the dough, the tomato sauce, the cheese and the vegetables yourself, it takes quite a long time. In fact, it seems rather ironic that such a slow food should nowadays be sold as fast food the world over.

On the other hand, there is something so more-ish about pizza that you can appreciate why someone would inevitably find ways to market it, and its components. Thanks to them, we are nowadays guaranteed our fill of pizza, in all sorts of flavours and shapes whenever we fancy, and for just as much work as we'd like to put in. Eating pizza can be as simple as dialling a number. But, looking beyond its cheesy exterior, pizza is neither simple, nor boring. You too can engage with its history, breeding and wit. You too can parent a pizza.

Pizza can be made with thin dough or fat dough, and with a little tomato sauce, a lot, or none at all. There are all sorts of cheeses and combinations of vegetables you can put on top. In fact you can design the pizza to suit your mood. When Ed Brown came to teach 'The Zen of Cooking' in 1998, he surprised us all by including bands of sautéed endive lettuce and roast carrots on his pizza—and leaving out the traditional tomato sauce entirely. It was magnificent! No surprise that he wooed his partner Patricia with such a pizza.

The recipe below, however, reverts to the traditional Schumacher style which many generations of participants have helped us to perfect. You can use this as a basis for your own experiments as you explore the slow but enjoyable art of making pizza from scratch.

Pizza Dough

For 4-5 (2 x 8" pizzas)	For 35-40
8 oz (225 g) white or 50% brown & 50% white flour	6 lb (2.7 kg)
1 tsp dried yeast or $^1/_4$ oz (5 g/$1^1/_2$ tsp) fresh yeast	$3^1/_2$ tbsp or 3 oz (75 g)
3 fl oz (85 ml/$^1/_3$ cup) warm water	$2^1/_2$ pints (1.4 litres/$1^1/_2$ US quarts)
1 tsp sugar	4 tbsp sugar
$^1/_2$ tsp salt	2 tbsp salt
1 tbsp olive oil	6 fl oz (150 ml/$^3/_4$ cup)
1 tsp sesame seeds (optional)	6 tbsp approx.
1 tsp dried oregano (optional)	6 tbsp approx.

1. If using the traditional active dried yeast, whisk this into the warm water and sugar. Leave for about 10 minutes in a warm place to froth up. (Further information on the different yeasts and how to handle them is given at the beginning of the bread-baking section.)

2. Combine flour, salt, olive oil, sesame seeds and oregano. If you are using fast-acting dried yeast, add this at this stage too. If you are using fresh yeast, crumble it in now. In both cases add the sugar as well. Add either the warm water or the frothed yeast mixture to the rest. Stir with a wooden spoon to begin with, then knead with your hands, once the water has been absorbed. Tip on to a lightly floured surface and knead until smooth and tacky but not sticky. If you have an electric mixer with a dough hook attachment, it will do all the kneading for you and the dough will form a smooth lump around the hook when ready.

3. Return to bowl and leave to rise for 45 minutes or until it doubles in size.

4. Knead again (this is called 'knocking back the dough', because all the bubbles get knocked out by your fists). The dough is now ready to be rolled out (see 'Assembling the Pizza').

Tomato Sauce for Pizza

What distinguishes this tomato sauce is the large amount of onions and the truly epicurean hint of anise.

For 4-6	For 35-40
2 large onions, finely sliced	4½ lb (2 kg)
3-6 cloves, fine chopped garlic	1 large head
½ tsp basil, thyme and oregano	2 tsp of each
large pinch ground anise seed	1-2 tsp
4 fl oz (110 ml/½ cup) red wine (optional)	1 pint (550 ml/2½ cups)
2 tbsp fine chopped fresh parsley	1-2 oz (25-55 g/½-1 cup)
8 oz (225 g/1 cup) can chopped tomatoes	2 lb (900 g)
4 oz (110 g/½ cup) tomato purée (paste)	1 lb (450 g)
olive oil for frying	olive oil for frying
salt and pepper to taste	1-2 tbsp salt, 1-2 tsp pepper

1. Sauté the onions and garlic in a little olive oil. Add salt, dried herbs, anise, and half the red wine. Cook until the onions are quite soft. Add the chopped tomatoes, purée and remaining wine. Continue cooking on a low flame until considerably reduced. Stir occasionally. This could take a long time!

2. Adjust seasoning and add parsley.

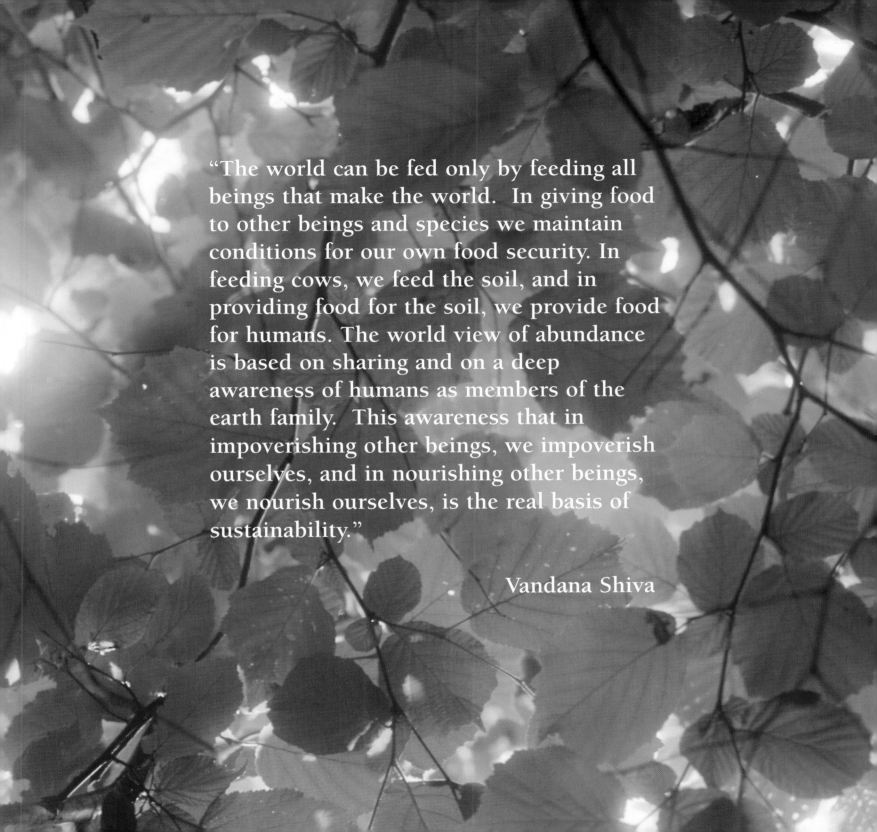

"The world can be fed only by feeding all beings that make the world. In giving food to other beings and species we maintain conditions for our own food security. In feeding cows, we feed the soil, and in providing food for the soil, we provide food for humans. The world view of abundance is based on sharing and on a deep awareness of humans as members of the earth family. This awareness that in impoverishing other beings, we impoverish ourselves, and in nourishing other beings, we nourish ourselves, is the real basis of sustainability."

Vandana Shiva

sheer volume of vegetables cooking on top of each other has a tendency to turn this dish into more of a stir-stew than stir-fry! To be on the safe side, allow 50 minutes cooking time when making the large quantity.

5. Add the mange-tout and cook for just a minute or two. Adding them just before serving time will ensure they are still bright green and slightly crisp when dished up.

6. Add the tempeh and the beansprouts, which are also nice when still a little crispy. Stir briefly, then add the prepared sauce, and cook for just as long as it takes to thicken (a minute or two).

7. Serve this vibrantly colourful stir-fry with brown rice or egg noodles.

Preparing Tempeh for Stir-fry

For 8-10	For 35-40
2 lb (900 g) tempeh	8 lb (3.6 kg)
2 fl oz (50 ml/¼ cup) tamari or soy sauce	12 fl oz (350 ml/1½ cups)
1 fl oz (25 ml/2-3 tbsp) orange juice	8 fl oz (225 ml/1 cup)
sunflower oil for frying	sunflower oil for frying

1. Tempeh usually comes in 9 oz (250 g) bricks that can be handled when defrosted (or even better, partially defrosted).

2. Cut the tempeh brick in ¾" (2 cm) cubes. These squares may prove more robust in a stir-fry, but you can also make ⅜" (1 cm) slices cut across the width, then halved.

3. Combine the tamari and orange juice, and pour over the tempeh. Stir very gently (and minimally) using a wooden spoon or your clean hands, until the liquid is evenly distributed (though not every patch has to be covered). Leave for 10-15 minutes to marinade, then strain. Reserve the liquid and add to the stir-fry sauce. (Soaking tempeh in re-heated tofu marinade also seems to work, and is one way of re-using this marinade once you've used it for tofu. If you do this, there is no need to add extra oil when baking the tofu.)

4. Deep fry tempeh in sunflower oil until crispy. This ensures that a fundamentally crumbly substance will have a good chance of staying in one piece. Alternatively, toss lightly in sunflower oil and bake in oven at 180°C (350°F, gas mark 4) for 20-30 minutes, gently turning half way through. (Spreading the tempeh in a single layer on non-stick baking parchment helps to prevent sticking and therefore crumbling.)

5. If using in a stir-fry, keep the prepared tempeh warm in a low oven until you're ready to combine it with other ingredients. No need to cover.

6. If you wish to use the tempeh as a cold snack or to make kebabs, include 1 tbsp/4 fl oz grated ginger when you marinade it, along with the soya sauce and orange. Sesame oil can also be used for frying and for cold snacks larger slices of tempeh can be made.

Stir-fry Sauce

For 8-10	For 35-40
8 fl oz (225 ml/1 cup) orange juice	30 fl oz (850 ml/5 cups)
4 fl oz (110 ml/1/2 cup) tamari/soya sauce	18 fl oz (1/2 litre/2 1/4 cups)
2 tbsp grated ginger approx.	5 oz (150 g/1 cup)
3-4 cloves garlic, crushed	10-15 approx.
2 tbsp honey	6 fl oz (175 ml/3/4 cup)
4 tsp toasted sesame oil	6 tbsp
4 tbsp cornflour	4 oz (110 g/1 cup)

1. Mix all ingredients together, except the cornflour.

2. Dissolve cornflour in a little water and whisk into the rest.

3. Add to sautéed vegetables towards end of cooking time. It will thicken very quickly and glaze the vegetables.

4. Serve with brown rice, white rice or egg noodles. Use nine 9 oz (250 g) packets of egg noodles for the larger quantity.

CLOCKWISE FROM TOP LEFT:
AVOCADO CORNUCOPIA
SPROUTING CARROT AND COURGETTE SALAD
FENNEL AND CHICORY SALAD WITH ORANGE
ANGELIC QUINOA SALAD

SALADS

Vinaigrette
Avocado Cornucopia
Harlequin Bean Salad
Sprouting Carrot and Courgette Salad
Cottage Cheese Serendipity
Fennel and Chicory Salad with Orange
Greek Gods' Everyday Salad
Leafy Green Salads
Warm Potato, Egg and Tomato Salad
Angelic Quinoa Salad
Indonesian Rice Salad
Popeye's Spinach Salad
Tabbouleh
Waldorf Salad
Tomato, Basil and Mozzarella Salad

VINAIGRETTE

Here's a simple French dressing for green salad, or any other vegetable or bean salad that needs dressing-up. Vary the amounts of honey, garlic, mustard, oil etc. to taste, and add some dried or fresh herbs if you fancy. There is plenty of room for creativity in vinaigrette making, and many kinds of vinegar, oil, mustard and seasonings to experiment with.

The quality of the ingredients is absolutely critical, so go for a good cold-pressed virgin olive oil (preferably organic) and red or white wine vinegar. Try raspberry, cider and tarragon vinegar for variation. Balsamic vinegar is really excellent and, though expensive, it's very strong, so you can use half as much vinegar in your dressing. A dressing made only with vinegar and no lemon will be more acid, and may require additional olive oil. Thus the ratio of vinegar to oil is 1 to 4, as opposed to 1 to 3 when you use lemon juice. For a lighter dressing, some people like to substitute sunflower oil for up to half the olive oil.

The smaller quantity given should be enough to dress a family bowl of about 1-2 lettuces, while the larger quantity will dress 2 or 3 very large bowls together containing 10-15 lettuces. This is a very rough guide, as lettuce size varies considerably—as does the amount of dressing people like to use.

8-12 servings

2 tbsp lemon juice
2 tbsp wine vinegar
  (or 4 tbsp of either lemon or vinegar)
8 tbsp ($\frac{1}{2}$ cup) olive oil
  (or use 4 tbsp olive
  and 6 tbsp organic sunflower oil)
2-3 tsp honey (or sugar)
1-2 tsp Dijon or grainy mustard
2-4 cloves garlic
1 pinch salt to taste
pinch black pepper, freshly ground

40-60 servings

$\frac{1}{4}$ pint (150 ml/$\frac{2}{3}$ cup)
$\frac{1}{4}$ pint (150 ml/$\frac{2}{3}$ cup)
  (or $\frac{1}{2}$ pint/300 ml of either)
1 pint (600 ml/$2\frac{1}{2}$ cups)
  (or 14 fl oz/400 ml/$1\frac{3}{4}$ cups olive
  and 6 fl oz/200 ml/$\frac{3}{4}$ cup sunflower)
2-4 tbsp
3 tbsp
4-8
$\frac{1}{2}$-1 tsp
$\frac{1}{2}$ tsp

1. Begin by combining the vinegar, lemon juice, mustard, honey, crushed garlic, herbs, salt and pepper. Whisk these together until smooth, using a fork or small wire hand whisk. The mustard and honey will dissolve more easily before the oil is added. (For larger amounts where a blender is used, this stage can be bypassed.)

2. Add the oil and whisk until completely integrated with other ingredients. An opaque, light brown liquid will form. For larger amounts, all ingredients (including roughly chopped garlic) can be combined in a liquidizer and blended in one go.

Consistency: sometimes the dressing will thicken substantially, and will stay emulsified (a bit like mayonnaise). At other times it separates and needs constant re-mixing. Either is OK, since some people like thinner dressings, whilst others prefer thicker.

3.   Dip a lettuce leaf in and taste, and adjust the ingredients until the vinaigrette tastes right to you. Salad dressing is a very personal thing, and some people are very fussy about it, preferring it one way or another: very acid, very oily, very garlicky, or with no mustard—or no honey.

4.   Toss green salad in vinaigrette only one minute before serving. Otherwise the delicate leaves will go dark and limp through absorbing the oil. The ratio of dressing to leaves is again a matter of personal preference, but if you have any doubts, dress your salad lightly and leave extra vinaigrette on one side.

5.   Extra vinaigrette can be stored in a jam jar with a tightly shutting lid. Shaking it up in this will be a very convenient way of re-mixing the oil and vinegar when you next need to dress a salad. No need to refrigerate, as oil, salt and vinegar are all preservatives. Olive oil will solidify in a cold place, and will need gently warming up.

AVOCADO CORNUCOPIA

This is one of the most luxurious salads you will probably ever find. It came to us from Sij, who first came to Schumacher College as a participant on Victor Papanek's course 'Design for the Real World' in 1991. If we constructed our human spaces like Sij built her salad, how delicious the world would be!

For 5-6	For 40
2-3 ripe (but not mushy) avocados	12-14
8 oz (225 g/1 small bunch) broccoli	4 lb (1.8 kg)
8 oz (225 g/1 medium 8"/20 cm long) courgette	4 lb (1.8 kg)
2 medium red peppers	8-10
8 oz (225 g/3 medium) tomatoes, firm, red and juicy	4 lb (1.8 kg)
2-3 fl oz (50-80 ml/$^1/_4$-$^1/_3$ cup) vinaigrette	1 pint (500 ml/2$^1/_2$ cups)
1 tbsp basil leaf (optional)	1 oz (25 g/$^1/_2$ cup)

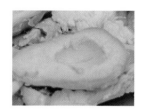

1. Slice the red peppers into 1" (2$^1/_2$ cm) square chunks. Massage generously in olive oil. Sprinkle with a little salt and roast in the oven at 180°C (350°F, gas mark 4) for 30 minutes or so until just going tender (but not browned). Stir after 15 minutes. Meanwhile cut the broccoli into bite-sized florets. As it is the florets that look particularly attractive in this salad, I usually keep the stem for another purpose.

2. Prepare some boiling salted water for blanching the broccoli and courgette (zucchini). Add the florets and return to the boil. Cook for a further 1-3 minutes, until the florets are bright green and possessing a pleasantly tender crunch—they easily turn a dingy khaki if they cook too long. Fish the broccoli out with a slotted spoon (so you can use the same water for the courgettes). Spread florets out to cool—if left in a pile, they will continue to cook each other. If at all overcooked, plunge briefly into cold water and drain. This stops the cooking process, but can make the vegetables too watery.

3. Cut the courgettes into round chunks (about $^1/_2$"/1-2 cm thick) and blanch briefly in the boiling water. They should, like the broccoli, be slightly *al dente*, and still bright in colour. Again, spread out and leave to cool. Then cut the tomatoes into chunks, or use whole cherry tomatoes (but beware of them skidding off plates).

4. Peel and slice avocadoes to obtain generous chunks. Toss in lemon juice to stop them going grey. Make vinaigrette including lemon (or orange) juice, balsamic vinegar, garlic, olive oil, etc.. Combine in a bowl, adding the delicate avocadoes and most of the torn or coarsely chopped basil last. Mix gently and minimally, with clean hands or a wooden spoon. Add more vinaigrette, salt and pepper if necessary. Sprinkle the remaining basil over the top. Alternatively serve on individual plates, sprinkle with basil and use as a starter.

HARLEQUIN BEAN SALAD

Here's a refreshing multi-coloured and multi-bean salad.

For 8	For 40
1^1/$_2$ oz (40 g/^{1}/$_4$ cup) chick peas	8 oz (225 g/1^1/$_4$ cups)
1^1/$_2$ oz (40 g/^{1}/$_4$ cup) red kidney beans	8 oz (225 g/1^1/$_4$ cups)
1^1/$_2$ oz (40 g/^{1}/$_4$ cup) flagelot beans	8 oz (225 g/1^1/$_4$ cups)
1^1/$_2$ oz (40 g/^{1}/$_4$ cup) butterbeans	8 oz (225 g/1^1/$_4$ cups)
10 oz (280 g) fine green beans	3 lb (1.4 kg)
6-8 spring onions	3 bunches
1 red and 1 yellow pepper (small)	3 red and 3 yellow (medium)
3-4 tbsp chopped parsley	3 oz (85 g/1^1/$_4$ cups)
approx. 4 fl oz (110 ml/^{1}/$_2$ cup) vinaigrette	1 pint (570 ml/2^1/$_2$ cups)

1.   Soak the chick peas, red kidney, flagelot and butterbeans separately in twice their depth of cold water overnight. Keeping them separate is important, as the different kinds of beans take different lengths of time to cook, and the red kidney beans would slightly discolour the others.

2.   Next morning cook the beans, each in separate saucepans of water. Cooking time will be 40-60 minutes. When ready, drain and leave to cool.

3.   Top and tail the green beans and cut into 1" (2^1/$_2$ cm) lengths. Cook briefly in boiling, salted water. Drain and leave to cool.

4.   Take the spring onions and remove any browning or yellowing outer leaves, roots and dry ends. Rinse. Chop up in ^{1}/$_4$" (^{1}/$_2$ cm) rings.

5.   Rinse and slice the red and yellow peppers into thin strips, 1" (2^1/$_2$ cm) long.

6.   Rinse and spin dry (or pat dry) the parsley. Chop finely.

7.   Make the vinaigrette (see vinaigrette recipe). A fairly sharp mixture probably complements the beans best, as they can be quite bland.

8.   The beans should all have cooled by the time you have completed the preparation of the other ingredients, so now you can combine everything in a bowl. Stir and taste. Adjust seasoning.

SPROUTING CARROT & COURGETTE SALAD

This crunchy carrot salad contains all sorts of nutritious treasure. The sprouts will need to be started about 3-4 days in advance (see pages 210-11), but if you forget, you can substitute with mung bean sprouts from your greengrocer.

For 6-8	For 35-40 plus
10 oz (275 g/2 cups) grated carrot	3 lb (1.4 kg)
8 oz (225 g/2 cups) grated courgette (zucchini)	2¹/₂ lb (1.1 kg)
3 tbsp roasted pumpkin seeds	6 oz (170 g/1¹/₄ cups)
3 tbsp roasted sunflower seeds	6 oz (170 g/1¹/₄ cups)
6 oz (170 g/1¹/₃ cups) sprouted green lentils or mung beans	2 lb (900 g/7 cups) or 8 oz (225 g/1²/₃ cups) before soaking
1 red pepper, finely sliced	4-5
3 oz (85 g/²/₃ cup) sweet corn (optional)	1¹/₄ lb (600 g)
4 fl oz (110 ml/¹/₂ cup) vinaigrette	1 pint (600 ml)

1. Scrub carrots (peel if necessary) and remove ends. Wash courgettes. Grate both vegetables coarsely.

2. Wash and slice peppers finely, cutting into approx. 1" inch (2 cm) strips. Rinse and drain the sprouts.

3. Spread the pumpkin and sunflower seeds on baking trays and roast for 8-10 minutes at 200°C (375°F, gas mark 4). It is extremely easy to forget these, so set a timer if you have one. Let them cool before adding to the rest.

4. Prepare vinaigrette (see page 108).

5. Sweetcorn: I usually only add corn when it is in season at our local organic farm, so this involves carving it off yesterday's leftover cobs. However, you could also use tinned sweet corn (drained); or frozen corn cooked with very little boiling water and a dash of olive oil, so that it semi-steams with a lid on.

6. Combine all ingredients in your salad bowl and dress with vinaigrette. There's no need to leave this until the very last moment, but bear in mind that preparing a raw salad hours in advance has no nutritious advantage: once sliced, or grated, vitamins and minerals start to leach out of the vegetables and crispness will also diminish. Sample the salad and adjust seasoning or quantity of vinaigrette if necessary.

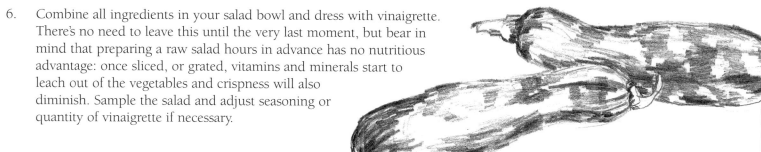

COTTAGE CHEESE SERENDIPITY

In this salad, crunchy vegetables and seeds are combined with soft cottage cheese to form a colourful blend of protein, fibre and fresh vitamins. To make a vegan version, substitute the cottage cheese with crumbled or diced tofu. Serve on its own, or with bread and soup.

For 6-8	For 40-45
1¼ lb (550 g/2½ cups) cottage cheese	8 lb (3.6 kg)
3 oz (85 g/⅔ cup) roasted cashew pieces	1½ lb (700 g)
2 tbsp toasted sesame seeds	4 oz (110 g/¾ cup)
7 oz (200 g/1¼ cups) sweet corn	2½ lb (1.1 kg)
1 medium carrot	6
2-3 spring onions	12-18
1 stalk celery	6
⅓ cucumber	2
4 tbsp chopped parsley	4 oz (110 g/1½ cups)
juice of half a lemon	3
pinch salt	1-2 tsp
pinch black pepper	½-1 tsp
watercress for garnishing	2 bunches

1. Wash the carrot, spring onion, celery and cucumber, and dice very small.

2. Spread the cashew pieces out on a baking tray and roast in a pre-heated oven (200°C/400°F, gas mark 5) for about 10 minutes until beginning to turn a pleasant golden brown. Likewise spread the sesame seeds out on another tray and toast in the oven for about the same amount of time, but check after 8 minutes as they may brown quicker than the cashews.

3. Carve the cooked sweetcorn off the cobs, if using fresh. Alternatively, cook frozen sweetcorn in a saucepan until tender—use a tiny bit of water and a knob of butter. Keep a lid on. If using tinned sweetcorn, simply drain off the liquid and use.

4. Mix all the prepared ingredients together. Check the seasoning and adjust.

5. Garnish with a ring of watercress and serve.

LEAFY GREEN SALADS

A hundred years ago, the idea of eating raw green leaves all year round would have been thought as absurd as landing on the moon. Nowadays, with polytunnels and the introduction of new varieties, it seems that we can go on growing salad leaves *ad infinitum*. And with central heating in our homes we don't have to boil our greens to feel warm inside. Spinach and cabbage themselves are often delicious when eaten raw in salad, and retain much more vitamin C this way.

Here at Schumacher College we have grown so addicted to our salads that we eagerly await the arrival of the little green leaves that come from Dartington market garden even in the depth of winter. These beautifully shaped, often rather exotic leaves include komitzuna, mizuna, purslane, rocket, pakchoi, lamb's cress and corn salad. They ripple with exciting tastes and textures of all sorts, and can be combined with regular lettuce if you want to dilute the effect. Not that lettuce is that 'regular' nowadays: it may be red and curly, or yellow and frizzy, indeed there are a multitude of different lettuce to choose from in every supermarket or green grocer. And if you have joined an organic vegetable box scheme, many varieties will doubtless choose you! They include standard round lettuce, plus Webbs, iceberg, little gem, lollo rosso, lollo bianco, frisée, cos, oakleaf, radicchio and many others.

Quantities

It is difficult to estimate how much lettuce you'll require, as lettuces and appetites for salad vary so enormously. However, a good rule of thumb is to think in terms of one 8 oz (225 g) lettuce per family of 4-6.

Ingredients

You'll need your lettuce or other tender green leaves as a base. To this you can add a whole variety of other raw vegetables, cut in whatever small shapes you like. These can include, for example, slices of carrot, tomato, red and green pepper, cucumber, cress, spring onion, mushroom, courgette (zucchini) and bean sprouts. Toasted pumpkin or sunflower seeds sprinkled on top can also make a delightfully nutty addition.

1. Cut off the stump of the root and carefully pull apart the leaves, taking care not to crush the lettuce. Cut any brown off the leaf base.

2. Many French people will insist you should wash the leaves whole. However, since the spinners operate much better with smaller pieces of leaf (larger ones tend to enclose the water, not letting it escape so readily), and it is easier to tear dry leaves, I usually tear them before rinsing. Tearing the leaves straight into the bowl you want to fill also enables you to judge the quantity accurately. Perhaps this method is particularly suitable when dealing with community quantities (see 5 below for tearing tips).

3. Whether torn or not, wash leaves lightly in a bowl of cold water, swishing them around to remove earth, slugs, snails, and anything else. If you find a particularly cute, intelligent snail please contact Gideon Kossoff, our

start flaking off. If fresh mint is available, plunge a generous bunch into the cooking water when potatoes are half way through cooking, for extra flavour.

3. Prepare the dressing, using a hand whisk or blender to combine all ingredients, and hopefully obtain a light emulsion.

4. Drain the potatoes and let them stand and drip in the colander for a few minutes. Then put them into a mixing bowl and pour the dressing over them. Gently stir with a wooden spoon until all the potatoes are coated.

5. Cut the tomatoes into generous pieces, compatible in size with your potatoes (or use cherry tomatoes whole or halved).

6. Peel the eggs—cracking and peeling them under cold water can make things easier. Halve about a quarter of the eggs lengthwise and reserve them on a plate for decorating the salad later on. Roughly chop the rest—making four to six pieces from each egg.

7. Chop the spring onions into approximately 1/4" (1/2 cm) rings. Put a few aside for garnishing.

8. Chop the parsley fairly finely. Reserve a little for garnishing.

9. Add the tomatoes, roughly chopped eggs, spring onions and parsley to the potatoes. Stir very gently (so that the egg does not become completely mashed in). Everything can be added to the potatoes when still warm—or even quite hot! Taste and add extra salt and pepper if needed.

10. Tip the salad into your serving bowl. Decorate with chopped parsley, spring onions, and a ring of egg halves around the edge. Avoid pressing the salad down: let it sit chunkily, even mountainously, with all its garnishes sprouting like wild plants on its surface. Finish off with a sprinkling of paprika if you like.

WALDORF SALAD

Simple to make, crunchy and refreshing, this fruity salad has been reinvented in many forms by many different cooks. Its first appearance, however, was probably on the menu of hotels owned by a certain Mr Waldorf—who also sponsored the creation of Rudolf Steiner's first progressive schools in Germany. In this recipe, the sharp crispness of apples and celery are complemented by the mellow crunch of toasted walnuts or pecans and the creamy bite of mayonnaise blended with lemon.

For 4-6	For 30
2 crisp medium eating apples	12
juice of half a lemon	2
4 sticks celery	4 pints (2.3 litres/2 good heads)
2 oz (55 g/½ cup) walnut or pecan halves	12 oz (350 g/3 cups)
mayonnaise (to taste)	1 pint (600 ml/2½ cups) approx.
1-2 pinches salt (to taste)	1-2 tsp
pinch freshly ground black pepper	½-1 tsp
watercress to garnish	2 bunches

1. Quarter, core and slice the apples into smallish chunks. Toss them in the lemon juice as you go, to prevent discolouring.

2. Wash and slice the celery thinly.

3. Toast the walnuts or pecans in the oven (180°C/350°F, gas mark 4) for 5-10 minutes until lightly browning. This will make them crunchier and more digestible. Reserve a few of the toasted halves to use as a garnish. Break or rough chop the rest.

4. Mix all the ingredients together and add mayonnaise to taste.

5. Season with pepper and salt as needed.

6. Clean the edge of the bowl or tip into a new bowl. Garnish with a ring of fresh, undressed watercress, and a scattering of the reserved walnuts.

ANGELIC QUINOA SALAD

This ancient Mayan grain was first introduced to Schumacher College by Anne Tarpy, who came as one of Seattle University's freelance students. Despite doing Master's credits and helping organize the soirées whilst she was here, Anne found time to do a lot of extra cooking. Quinoa (pronounced "keenwa") is reputed to be a complete source of protein, so it is not surprising that when you look carefully at the individual grains, you'll notice that each wears a tiny white halo.

Quinoa can be eaten hot or cold. In this recipe, we've combined it with various crunchy vegetables, some juicy sultanas and roast cashews. I have always been surprised that such an unfamiliar grain has been received so well, even by our more stoic English customers, so why not try it as an angelic alternative to rice salad or tabbouleh?

For 6-8	For 40-45
8 oz (225 g/1¼ cups) quinoa	2 lb 12 oz (1.3 kg)
15 fl oz (425 ml/2 cups) boiling water	4½ pints (2.5 litres/2¾ US quarts)
1 tsp dried mint	2 tbsp
1 tsp salt approx.	1-2 tbsp approx.
2 fl oz (55 ml/¼ cup) lemon juice	12 fl oz (350 ml/1½ cups)
1 large clove garlic, crushed	2 tbsp
2 sticks celery, finely sliced	1 head
2" (3 cm) of cucumber, small diced	1 large cucumber
4 oz (110 g/¾ cup) carrot, finely diced	1½ lb (700 g/5 cups)
4-5 spring onions, chopped	2-3 bunches
2 oz (55 g/½ cup) cashew pieces, dry-roast	12 oz (350 g/3 cups)
3-4 tbsp sultanas	7 oz (200 g/1¼ cups)
4-6 tbsp (¼ cup) freshly chopped parsley	5 oz (140 g/2 cups)
3-4 tbsp olive oil	10 fl oz (300 ml/1¼ cups)

1. Combine the quinoa with the boiling water in an ovenproof bowl. Stir in the mint. Cover with aluminium foil or a tight-fitting lid and leave in a moderate oven (170°C, 325°F, gas mark 3) for about 30 minutes, or until all the water has been absorbed. Give it a stir half way through cooking time so the surface grains don't dry out. When cooked all the grains should be soft, but still separate (when overcooked, they begin to stick together). Remove from oven.

2. Stir the lemon juice, garlic and oil into the quinoa, and allow to cool. Spread the cashews out on a baking tray and roast in the oven at about 180°C (325°C, gas mark 4) for 8 minutes. Prepare the remaining ingredients and add to the quinoa. Check the seasoning and adjust if necessary.

Mint

part used: leaf

INDONESIAN RICE SALAD

This spicy brown rice salad involves a lot of intricate toasting, chopping and mixing. It's well worth the effort, and has proved a favourite weekend salad for many years, bejewelled as it is with exotic flavours and goodness of all sorts—including dried fruit, toasted nuts and crisp pepper slices. Be careful when you add the chilli: add a little at a time and taste in between!

The original recipe and dressing came from the Moosewood Cookbook—and included water chestnuts. This beautifully handscripted cookbook features many delicious and creative vegetarian dishes evolved by Mollie Katzen and served at the famous Moosewood Restaurant at Ithaca, New York.

For 6-10	For 40 plus
To Cook	
8 oz (225 g/1 heaped cup) raw brown rice	3 lb 12 oz (1.7 kg)
14 fl oz (400 ml/1¾ cups) water	5¼ pints (3 litres/3 US quarts + ½ cup)
Dressing	
1½ tbsp peanut oil	6 fl oz (170 ml/¾ cup)
1½ tbsp toasted sesame oil	6 fl oz (170 ml/¾ cup)
5 tbsp orange juice	15 fl oz (400 ml/2 cups)
2-4 cloves garlic, crushed	6-10
¼ tsp crushed fresh red chilli to taste	1-2 tsp
1 tbsp soy sauce	4 fl oz (110 ml/½ cup)
1 tbsp cider vinegar	4 fl oz (110 ml/½ cup)
Add	
5 tbsp raisins	15 fl oz (400 ml/2 cups)
Toast	
5 tbsp toasted red skin peanuts	10 oz (275 g/2½ cups)
5 tbsp toasted cashew pieces	10 oz (275 g/2½ cups)
Chop	
5 dried apricots (preferably unsulphured)	10 oz (275 g/2 cups)
4 spring onions, narrow rings	16 approx.
1 stalk celery, fine slices	8 stalks
1 medium red pepper, smallish slices	4-6
1 narrow carrot, sliced in thin rings	6-8 (depending on size)

Garnish
edge with a ring of watercress or lettuce, as available.

4. Chop the spring onion into narrow ¼" (½ cm) rings, discarding any brown or dry parts. If using red onion, peel and slice very finely.

5. Using your fingers lightly, tear the basil leaves carefully into smallish pieces or rough chop, according to your taste. However, don't chop too small as basil bruises easily and becomes dark green and wet.

6. Halve the black olives, removing stones if necessary (if pitted, you can use whole).

7. Halve the avocadoes lengthways, peel and remove any browning areas. Slice into longish pieces. Drizzle with a little lemon juice to help prevent discoloration.

8. Now all the ingredients are ready, so you can begin layering them into an attractive dish. Begin with a layer of tomatoes (mixing the colours if you have multicoloured tomatoes). Next comes a sprinkling of spring onion, black olive and basil; a few slices of avocado, several pieces of mozzarella, a pinch of salt and black pepper—and finally a dash of balsamic vinegar followed by a somewhat more generous splashing of olive oil.

Continue with the layering until you have used up all the ingredients, but remember to make sure you have some mozzarella, avocado, olives, onions and basil left to decorate the top with—make your previous layer thinner if you think you might be running out.

9. Variations: the avocado and mozzarella can be left out.

Ed Brown and participants in 'The Zen of Cooking' course in September 1998

PATÉS & DIPS

Houmous

Coriander & Butter Bean Paté

Chestnut & Red Pepper Spread

Mushroom & Cream Cheese Spread

Guacamole

Fresh Tomato Salsa

Tzatziki

Vegan Almond Mayonnaise

INTRODUCTION TO PATÉS AND DIPS

This short section deals with the rich, savoury, mousse-like mouthfuls that we so often serve at lunch time as an alternative to cheese. On these occasions, dips and patés accompany soup, bread and salads—but they can also be served with crispbreads, and as dips for vegetable crudités.

I have found it difficult to find elegant words to describe the consistency you aim to obtain when blending chick peas for houmous, or chestnuts for red pepper spread. Words like mushy, mashy, slushy, sloppy, porridgey and gloopy, all make these lovely dips sound like baby food. But never mind—maybe that is why everyone likes them so much!

The main thing to remember is that when blending these patés or dips, you are aiming to create a substance that can be heaped onto a crispbread without running off, or be stuffed into a pitta bread without oozing out. Equally, you should be able to dip a stick of carrot or celery in and lift it to your mouth, without the mixture dropping on to the table.

If you do not have an electric blender to pulverize your beans, it is especially important to ensure the beans are very soft when cooked, as you will have to mash them instead, rub them through a sieve, or employ some other special technique you may have developed.

HOUMOUS

Houmous (or hummus) is one of the best known Middle Eastern cold dips. It goes well with pitta bread, tabbouleh, green salads, or as a dip served with taco chips and raw vegetable sticks.

Traditional recipes vary in the amount of lemon juice, garlic and tahini used. A little freshly-ground cumin powder blended into the cooked chick peas provides another authentic variation. I have also experimented with adding a little honey and Dijon mustard, which seems to give a pleasant enhancement of flavours; and I often add orange juice instead of more chick pea water or oil, to achieve the right consistency without losing flavour. (Chick peas are also commonly known as garbanzo beans.)

For 6-8	For 40-45
8 oz (225 g/1½ cups) chick peas, soaked overnight	3 lb (1.4 kg)
2-3 cloves garlic, crushed	12-18
3 tbsp tahini approx.	9 fl oz (250 ml/1 generous cup)
4 tbsp olive oil	12 fl oz (350 ml/1½ cups)
3 tbsp lemon juice	8 fl oz (225 ml/1 cup)
2 tbsp orange juice	4 fl oz (100 ml/½ cup)
1-2 fl oz (25-50 ml/2-4 tbsp) chick pea water	5-10 fl oz (150-300 ml/½-1¼ cups)
½ tsp ground cumin (optional)	2-3 tsp
salt and pepper (to taste)	1-3 tsp salt, 1 tsp pepper
garnish: black olives, paprika, olive oil	

1. Drain the chick peas and cover with fresh water. Bring to the boil then simmer until very soft (about 1½ to 2½ hours). Remove any foam that forms with a perforated spoon. Use a pressure cooker if available, to reduce cooking time.

2. Tip into a colander and drain, reserving the liquid. Leave chick peas to cool.

3. Blend (or mash) the chick peas with the remaining ingredients. Add more lemon juice if necessary, and include enough of the reserved liquid (or orange juice) to give a soft dropping consistency, not too runny. It is a good idea to add the liquids little by little, as the amount needed will mysteriously vary with each batch of chick peas.

4. Adjust the seasoning. Add a little freshly ground cumin if you like (toasting this lightly in a dry pan before grinding will help to bring out the aroma).

5. Garnish with a sprinkling of paprika, a significantly placed black olive or two and a drizzling of olive oil.

CORIANDER & BUTTER BEAN PATÉ

This pleasant light green bean paté makes a nice alternative to houmous. Vary the amount of fresh coriander according to taste, and depending on your budget.

For 6-8 servings	For 35-40
6 oz (175 g/1 cup) butter beans (dry weight), soaked (use double quantity if using tinned)	2 lb (900 g)
2 tsp vegetable stock powder	3 tbsp
2-3 cloves of garlic, crushed	8-10
½-1 oz (10-25 g/¼-½ cup) chopped fresh coriander leaves	2-4 oz (50-110 g/1-2 cups)
1-2 tbsp finely chopped fresh parsley	½-¾ oz (10-20 g/⅓ cup)
juice of ½ lemon (to taste)	juice of 3-4
1-2 tbsp light tahini (optional)	3-4 fl oz (100 ml/½ cup)
pinch salt	2-3 tsp
pinch pepper	1-2 tsp
½ tsp ground coriander seed (to taste)	1-2 tsp
1 tsp Dijon mustard	2-3 tbsp
2-3 tbsp olive oil	4-6 fl oz (150 ml/½-¾ cup)

1. Soak beans overnight.

2. Cook beans (approx. 1 hour). Add the vegetable stock powder/cubes half way through cooking and continue. Reserve a few of the cooked butter beans on a saucer for decorating the finished paté.

3. Wash, spin or pat dry and chop the parsley and coriander leaves. Reserve a few of the coriander leaves whole or rough chopped for garnishing later on. Chop the rest of the leaves very finely.

4. Grind the coriander seed in a coffee/spice grinder or in a pestle and mortar. It may be necessary to prepare a larger quantity in the grinder, and just take what you need. (This is in order to cover the blade, rather than just have it whizzing over the top of the seeds. Keep surplus ground coriander in a screw of foil/cling film for another time.)

5. Blend together all ingredients. Add some more olive oil, lemon juice, orange juice or bean water if you need extra moisture to achieve the desired consistency. Taste and adjust seasoning. Garnish with the reserved coriander leaves and butter beans.

WENDY'S APRICOT HAZELNUT TORTE

Once upon a time, many years ago, somebody somewhere baked a delicious apricot tart using instructions that came from the back of a sugar packet. Tasting this, Wendy Cook realized the recipe had great potential and tried to recreate the concoction using the hazelnuts, apricots and oranges that grow abundantly in Majorca. After several dinner parties on her sunny Mediterranean terrace, she had the recipe near enough perfect. Her guests would not leave.

Arriving at the College, Wendy soon commented that the only thing lacking was an abundance of desserts. They help us feel connected with the heavenly realms, she said. One slice of this delicious torte, adorned with a dollop of clotted cream, and you will feel well satisfied, convinced that this is the food of angels, and that angels are a little more earthy than you had ever imagined.

1 x 11" torte (serves 12-16 people)	2 tortes (serves approx. 30)
Base	
6 oz (170 g/1½ cups) roasted hazelnuts	12 oz (350 g/3 cups)
4 oz (110 g/1 scant cup) flour (unbleached white or 85% brown)	8 oz (220 g/1¾ cups)
3 oz (85 g/6 heaped tbsp) muscovado sugar	6 oz (175 g/1 cup)
6 oz (175 g/1½ sticks) butter	12 oz (350 g/3 sticks)
2 tbsp cold water	4 tbsp
Filling	
1 lb (500 g) soaked, stewed, dried apricots	2 lb (900 g)
zest and juice of 1 organic orange	2
2 oz (55 g/4 heaped tbsp muscovado sugar)	4 oz (110 g/²/₃ cup)
Topping	
4 oz (110 g/1 scant cup) flour (unbleached white or 85% brown)	8 oz (220 g/1¾ cups)
4 oz (110 g/1 stick) butter	8 oz (220 g/2 sticks)
4 oz (110 g/½ heaped cup) muscovado sugar	8 oz (220 g/1¼ cups)
2 tsp freshly ground or powdered cinnamon	4 tsp

1. Soak the apricots overnight in boiling water with strips of orange zest. To obtain the zest strips, peel the orange carefully, avoiding the bitter white pith. Slice the rind in roughly ¼" (½ cm) strips.

2. Next day, cook the apricots and zest with sugar and orange juice (using the amounts listed under 'Filling'). Continue cooking until tender and the liquid has become syrupy and mostly been absorbed by the apricots.

3. To preparing the hazelnuts for the base, firstly roast them in a moderate to hot oven for 5-10 minutes until they are golden brown and the skins beginning to flake off. When they have cooled a little, rub them between your hands to remove loose skins. Toss them in a colander, outside the house, and let the loosened skins fly away. Grind them up in your food processor.

4. Now continue preparing the base by mixing together the ground hazelnuts and other dry ingredients. Rub in the butter until a fine breadcrumb texture is obtained. Add a little cold water to bind. Pat into a layer on the bottom of a buttered loose-bottomed flan tin.

5. Prepare the topping by rubbing the butter lightly into the dry ingredients until you have a fine crumb texture.

6. Now assemble the torte by spreading the apricots on top of the base and sprinkling the topping on top of them. Gently press down.

7. Bake in a pre-heated moderate oven for about 50 minutes or until golden brown (180°C, 350°F, gas mark 4). Serve warm or cold, with cream.

BRAZILIAN BANANAS

There is something very distinctive about a banana baked with a little fresh citrus juice, a dab of butter and some fresh coconut. If you can't get the fresh coconut or desiccated flakes, try flaked almonds, or leave the bananas blissfully unadorned. Delicious as a light dessert served warm with vanilla ice cream, frozen yoghurt or whipped cream.

Serves 4-6	For 25-30
5 medium bananas	30
4 fl oz (110 ml/$^1/_2$ cup) fresh orange juice	24 fl oz (700 ml/3 cups)
1 tbsp fresh lemon juice	3 fl oz (100 ml/$^1/_3$ cup)
pinch salt	$^1/_2$ tsp
$^1/_2$ oz (10 g/1 tbsp) butter	3 oz (85 g/$^3/_4$ stick) approx.
1$^1/_2$ oz (40 g/$^1/_2$ cup) grated fresh coconut	8 oz (225 g/2$^1/_2$ cups)

1. Peel the bananas and cut lengthwise into halves.

2. Place in a buttered ovenproof dish.

3. Combine the juices and salt and pour over the bananas.

4. Dot with butter. Cover and bake at 180°C (350°F, gas mark 4) for 30-40 minutes, until the bananas have undergone a textural transformation and deepened in colour.

5. If fresh coconut is not available, sprinkle desiccated coconut or flaked almonds over the bananas for the last 5 minutes of cooking, to allow a slight toasting.

6. If freshly grated coconut is available, sprinkle over the bananas when they are ready to serve.

JAMAICAN CHOCOLATE MOUSSE TORTE

If you have ever felt that chocolate mousse is really a little too fluffy, you may enjoy trying it again in a rather different form. In this recipe, a ginger biscuit crust is made, filled with chocolate mousse, and then refrigerated until set. After a couple of hours the dessert will be ready to slice. The combination of smooth, aerated chocolate mousse and crunchy, slightly chewy, gingernut crust makes indulging in chocolate mousse an altogether more satisfying textural experience.

Serves 6-8	Serves 35-40
1 x 8" (20 cm) deep loose-bottomed flan tin	3 x 11" (27 cm)
Crust	
10 oz (280g/2½ cups) crushed gingernut biscuits	3 lb (1.35 kg)
2½ oz (60 g/½ stick + 1 tbsp) butter, melted	12 oz (340 g/3 sticks)
4 tsp golden syrup	4 fl oz (110 ml/½ cup)
½ tsp ginger powder	1½ tsp
Mousse	
7 oz (200 g) plain dark chocolate	1 lb 9 oz (700 g)
3 tbsp brandy	6 fl oz (175 ml/¾ cup)
7 eggs	30
or 4 eggs + 5 fl oz (140 ml/⅔ cup) double/whipping cream	or 20 eggs + 25 fl oz (700 ml)
Decoration	
2 fl oz (55 ml/¼ cup) whipping cream, approx.	1 pint (550 ml/2½ cups) approx.
a few pieces of crystallized ginger	1 oz (25 g/2 tbsp) approx.

1. Begin by very lightly oiling with sunflower oil the tins you will be using. Tins should have detachable bottoms and ideally be about 1½" (4 cm) deep.

2. Crush the gingernut biscuits until a fine crumb texture is obtained. You can do this in your food processor with the knife attachment or with a rolling pin.

3. Gently melt the butter and golden syrup in a saucepan.

4. Add the biscuit crumbs and ginger powder to the melted butter and stir thoroughly.

5. Sprinkle some of the crumbs over the bottom of the tin, about $^{1}/_{4}$" ($^{1}/_{2}$ cm) thick. Press down a little with the back of a metal spoon. You will also need to create walls—a little more difficult, but you soon get the knack. Sprinkle more crumbs around the inside edge of the tin. Again, use the spoon to press the walls and build them up to about 1-1$^{1}/_{2}$" (2-3 cm). Once you have created the case, bake it for a mere 4-5 minutes in a pre-heated moderate oven. If you bake it for much longer, the crust can become too stiff when cool, and you'll have to endure the anguish of watching your guests hammering their dessert with a spoon. Leave to cool.

6. Gently melt the chocolate in a double boiler (see Brownies recipe, point 1). Don't stir it. Pour the brandy on to the melting chocolate and leave it to warm up a bit. Stir in when all the chocolate is melted. (Stirring cold liquids into warm melted chocolate can sometimes cause it to stiffen in a peculiar way.)

7. Separate the eggs and stir the yolks into the warm (but not very hot) chocolate mixture.

8. Whisk the egg whites until smooth white peaks reminiscent of ocean surf are formed. Sometimes people ask me whether it's possible to over-whip egg whites: the answer is that in the case of mousse, it is. Over-whipped whites take on the appearance of being almost dry and slightly grainy, like foam stuffing. As a result you will get little white specks showing on top of the mousse, but this isn't too serious.

9. The chocolate/yolk/brandy mixture should by now have cooled to almost room temperature, so carefully fold the whipped egg whites into it—do not beat. (If substituting cream for some of the eggs, carefully whip the cream—see 11 below. Fold this into the chocolate mixture before adding the whipped egg whites.)

10. Pour the chocolate mousse mixture into the ginger biscuit cases. Leave in the fridge to set for a couple of hours or overnight.

11. Before serving, remove the edges of the tins. Decorate with translucent slices of crystallized ginger and whipped cream piped around the edge. Again, be careful not to over-whip the cream: whip it just enough so that it will hold an impression. Alternatively, serve single cream with the mousse, or leave it out altogether.

ANGELA AND GRAHAM'S FRESH FRUIT PAVLOVA

Angela Bein first came to Schumacher on Rupert Sheldrake's course in 1991. She was soon joined by her partner Graham Griffin, and with him began to hatch a plan to transform the abandoned swimming pool at the Old Postern into a sunken garden. The next six months were spent intricately lining the crude blue walls of the pool with beautiful granite stone-walling, creating half-moon flower beds and even a waterfall.

When Angela and Graham eventually returned to Tasmania to build themselves an elegant mudbrick house, they left behind not only a beautiful garden-sanctuary that grows more entrancing by the years, but a recipe for a spectacular meringue-based dessert which can be made in a comparative twinkling of the eye.

Seasonal soft fruit such as raspberries, blackberries and strawberries can, of course, be used as an equally delicious substitute for the original, rather exotic combination of fresh fruit given here.

For 10-15	For 35-40
Meringue	
8 egg whites	24 egg whites
1 lb (450 g/2½ cups) brown sugar	3 lb (1.4 kg)
4 tsp cider vinegar	4 tbsp
2 tsp arrowroot	2 tbsp
Filling	
1 pint (600 ml/2½ cups) double cream, whipped	3 pints (1.7 litres/7 cups)
2 lb (900 g/5 cups) fresh fruit approx.	6 lb (3.2 kg/3 US quarts) approx.
e.g. ⅓ pineapple, 3 kiwifruit	e.g. 1 pineapple, 9 kiwifruit
3 passion fruit or small ripe mango	10 passion fruit or 2 small mango
2 bananas & 8 oz (250 g) strawberries	8 bananas & 1½ lb (700 g) strawberries
optional: chocolate flakes or	optional: chocolate flakes or
flaked almonds to sprinkle over	flaked almonds to sprinkle over

1.   Whisk egg whites until stiff white peaks are formed. (Although Angela and Graham managed to complete their beautiful house entirely without power tools, an electric egg whisk is definitely recommended here, especially for the larger quantity.)

2.   Whisk in sugar, a little at a time.

3. Whisk in vinegar and arrowroot (if available).

4. Prepare 1-3 12" (30 cm) baking sheets as follows. Line with baking parchment or greaseproof paper, coat thinly with sunflower oil and dust with cornflour, using a sieve. This will stop the meringue sticking.

5. Using a large metal spoon, swiftly shape the thick meringue mixture into 1-3 large open nests with roughly 1" (2 cm) bottoms and meringue mounded up around the edges.

6. Bake at 120°C (250°F, gas mark ½) for 1 hour until dry and crispy on the outside and slightly chewy in the middle. The meringue will feel quite strong and brittle to touch, and sound hollow if you tap it.

7. Leave to cool, and then move to a decorative plate or board if you have one big enough.

8. Peel and slice the large fruit into smallish pieces. Slice the strawberries as necessary. (Avoid rinsing the soft fruit if possible, as it may get too watery. Drain it well if you do have to rinse it, or pat dry.) Mix fruit together with the cream.

9. Whip the double (or whipping) cream until it is thick enough to hold an impression, but not grainy. Be very careful once it starts to thicken. If over-whipped, it can separate and turn into whey and butter.

10. Two ways of putting the pavlova together:

(a) simply fill with the whipped cream and then the fresh fruit. Or,

(b) line the meringue nest with half the cream. Pile the fruit on top and hide it like buried treasure under a second layer of whipped cream. Decorate the top with flakes of grated/peeled chocolate, a sprinkling of flaked almonds, and even a few tell-tale pieces of fruit.

PEARS POACHED IN WHITE WINE & BLACKCURRANT

The almost opalescent glow and soft granular texture of whole poached pears makes a unique light dessert that can be served hot or cold, with cream, crême fraiche or ice cream. Pears can be poached in various fruity or alcoholic liquids, red wine, white wine, orange juice, brandy, port—even the remainder of your Christmas punch will do. The creamy flesh of the pear will take on the colour of the syrup, so if you want deep pink pears use red wine, if you want sunset-orange pears, use a mixture of white wine and orange juice.

In this recipe a mixture of organic blackcurrant cordial, white wine, honey, sugar, cinnamon quills and citrus rind is used, diluted with a little water. This results in delicious purply-brown pears, with a very distinct flavour.

For 4-6	For 35-40
6 good size firm pears	35-40
10 fl oz (280 ml/1¼ cups) white wine (medium/sweet)	1½ pints (850 ml/3½ cups)
6 fl oz (175 ml/¾ cup) concentrated blackcurrant cordial	1 pint (550 ml/2½ cups)
4 fl oz (110 ml/½ cup) water	15 fl oz (400 ml/2 cups)
4 oz (110 g/½ cup) golden granulated sugar	14 oz (400 g/2 cups)
6 tbsp honey	7 fl oz (200 ml/1 cup)
rind of an organic lemon	3
rind of an organic orange	3
1 cinnamon quill	3-4

1. Peel the pears. Keep whole and leave the stalk on. Rinse if necessary. Place them in a fairly deep, lidded ovenproof dish. Then combine all the other ingredients in a saucepan and gently bring to the boil, stirring occasionally.

2. Thread the citrus rind and cinnamon quills between the pears, and pour the hot syrup over them. Put the lid on. Bake slowly in a low oven (150°C/300°F, gas mark 2) for 1½-2½ hours. After about 40 minutes, carefully turn the pears with a wooden spoon, so that any exposed surfaces get a chance to marinade in the syrup. When ready, the pears will be tender.

3. The pears can be served hot or cold. If serving cold you may wish to transfer them to a glass dish and remove the cinnamon and part of the liquid (which can be served as a drink). Some people reduce the liquid to make a much thicker syrup, and then pour it over the pears.

PLUM TART
WITH ALMOND CRUST

Somewhere in the garden of Schumacher College a plum tree is hiding, forbidden territory to participants because you have to cross a neighbour's lawn to find it. Every few years, the tree has a bumper crop. Bernadette, our neighbour, says the men in her life (three sons and a husband) won't eat plums. Nor will the cat, the cockerel or the ferret. So we arrange picking expeditions and try to think up different things to do with plums. Here is one simple recipe we've come up with, where the fruit needs no pre-cooking.

For 1 x 10" (25 cm) round flan tin	For 4 x 10" (25 cm) flan tins

Pastry

6 oz (170 g/1¼ cups) plain flour	1 lb 8 oz (700 g)
1 oz (25 g/3 tbsp) caster sugar	4 oz (110 g/½ cup)
pinch salt	½ tsp
2 oz (55 g/½ cup) ground almonds	8 oz (225 g/2½ cups)
3 oz (85 g/¾ stick) butter	12 oz (350 g/4 sticks)
1 tsp cinnamon powder or mixed spice	4 tbsp
2 tbsp sunflower oil	4 fl oz (125 ml/½ cup)
a little milk to bind	a little more

Filling

2 lb (900 g) Victoria plums approx.	8 lb (3½ kg)
2 oz (55 g/½ cup) semolina to sprinkle, approx.	up to 8 oz (225 g/2 cups)
2-4 tbsp brown sugar, to taste	up to 8 oz (225 g/1 cup)
3 tbsp clear honey or golden syrup	up to 8 fl oz (225 ml/1 cup)

1. Cut the butter into the flour. Leave in a warmish place to soften.

2. Add salt, cinnamon, sugar and ground almonds. Rub in the butter with your fingertips until it is thoroughly distributed, giving a breadcrumb-like appearance.

3. Add the sunflower oil and enough milk to allow all ingredients to join together as a soft, but not sticky dough.

4. Divide pastry in three if making the large quantity. Roll out each dough-ball on a floured surface with a rolling pin to obtain a large, thin circle that matches your tin size. Roll this lightly around your rolling pin and unroll it carefully over the oiled tin. Gently press it into the edges of the tin, making sure not to stretch it. Cut off surplus pastry. Flute the crust-edge with fingers/fork if you like. (This pastry is quite short, so patchwork it together if you find it difficult to lift in one piece).

5. Wash, halve and de-stone the Victoria plums. Taste to see how sweet they are and therefore how much brown sugar to use.

6. To work out how many plums to use for the decorative top layer of the tart, lightly place them in the pastry case/s, selecting the best halves, until you have one layer of plum halves all touching each other. The remaining plums can be sliced up—they will become the bottom layer. Therefore you need to remove the plums you've put in the case/s, and keep them on one side for later.

7. Sprinkle about a third of the semolina generously over the bottom of the pastry case/s. This will help absorb some of the plum juice, and prevent the flan bottom from going soggy. Next arrange a layer of plum slices on top of this. Sprinkle some more semolina and some brown sugar over these. Make another layer of sliced plums, brown sugar and semolina if you still have some left (it will depend upon the size of the plums). Finish by arranging the reserved plum halves, cut side down on top of a brown sugar and semolina layer.

8. Drizzle golden syrup or honey over the decorative top layer of plums.

9. Bake at 180°C (350°F, gas mark 4) for 40-60 minutes until crust is golden brown. The semolina will swell, absorbing some of the juices.

10. Serve warm or cold with cream, ice cream or yoghurt.

YOGHURT FRUIT SALAD

This is an incredibly simple dessert to whip up at the last moment. Basically it's a variation on standard fruit yoghurt—such as you might find in dainty little cartons at your local shop. But you begin with plain yoghurt and make it fruity in two ways—first by adding a little jam, and secondly by adding a little chopped fresh fruit. Sometimes chopped dried fruit (dates, apricots, figs) are added too. The variations are endless: you can mix many fruits and garnish with roast chopped nuts, or you can home in on a single seasonal soft fruit (raspberry, strawberry, etc.) and match the jam. Here is an example of a more mixed brew of yoghurt fruit salad.

For about 4 people	For about 40
1 pint (600 ml/2½ cups) natural yoghurt	10 pints (5.7 litres/6 US quarts)
1 eating apple, cored & chopped	10
1 banana, sliced	10
1-2 apricots or peaches (if available)	10-15
2 oz (55 g/⅓ cup) dates, chopped small	1 lb 2 oz (500 g/3½ cups)
4 oz (110 g/½ cup) good quality jam (apricot, black cherry, strawberry etc.)	2½ lb (1.1 kg/5 cups)

1. Using a fork, blend the jam with a little of the yoghurt to break up any jelly-like lumps. Add rest of yoghurt and stir. This is the base to which you can add your chosen fruits. Taste to see if the mixture is sweet enough and blend in a little more jam if necessary. (A liquidizer should not be used for this process, as it can make the mixture become too runny).

2. Cut the fresh fruit up into small pieces. (Only fruit that you would enjoy eating raw should be chosen, and it is better to avoid very watery fruits like oranges.)

3. Finely chop the dates and put some on one side to use as a garnish.

4. Stir the fruit and most of the dates into the yoghurt mixture. Pour into individual bowls or a large bowl. Top with a sprinkling of chopped dates.

A SELECTION OF COOKIES, INCLUDING
GINGER CRUMBLE SLICE
ALMOND SESAME BISCUITS
SHORTBREAD
COCONUT ISLAND MUNCHABLES
TWEET TWEET COOKIES
CAROB COOKIES
CHOC-CHIP AND HAZELNUT COOKIES
PEANUT CRUNCHETTES

BISCUITS

Carob Cookies
Choc-Chip and Hazelnut Cookies
Coconut Island Munchables
Flapjacks
Honey and Lemon Cookies
Ginger Crumble Slice
Peanut Crunchettes
Shortbread
Tweet Tweet Cookies
Almond Sesame Biscuits

SOME COOKIE NOTES

The following section contains several recipes for what people in the United Kingdom call biscuits. At least we used to call them biscuits. Nowadays it seems the word 'cookie' is taking over—and when you say 'biscuit' to Americans, they say it means something else. Whatever you call them, the most important thing about a biscuit or a cookie is that it's not a 'cake'.

Storage Most biscuits (though perhaps not all cookies) should have a texture that is short, crisp and crumbly. This dryness is what enables them to keep so well (up to a month) when stored in an airtight container with only other biscuits for company. If you put biscuits into a tin with cakes, which are much moister entities, the biscuits will become moist too—and chewy.

Ingredients In all recipes, I recommend using unbleached organic plain white flour (unless otherwise stated). Sometimes I use half organic brown flour instead, or maybe three-quarters, but rarely 100% as it can make biscuits (as well as cake and bread) rather heavy. I also use free-range eggs and, when possible, organic sugar, butter and nuts. Many of the recipes suggest using muscovado sugar—this is a soft, moist brown sugar that comes in light and dark shades. It usually contains lumps and needs to be sieved. If not available, substitute with any other sugar of your choice. If you need to avoid butter, use a non-hydrogenated margarine instead. If it is marked as suitable for cooking, it will work fine in all the recipes, though the result may not be quite so crispy. Avoid low-fat margarines, which may contain extra water. Butter is preferred as it is a less highly processed ingredient, and is considered to produce more delicious results.

Cooking times When embarking on biscuit making, you are involving yourself in preparing one of the fastest-cooking of all tea-time snacks. You have to be vigilant, to make sure they don't remain too long in the oven and overcook. But don't give up if you do burn a batch of biscuits: it happens to us all occasionally. Try using a timer, and avoid starting to do anything else until they are ready. Cultivate the feeling of being 'on edge' when there's something in the oven that might need your attention!

Shaping and freezing cookie dough In most recipes where cookies are individually formed into circles (as opposed to baked in a slab and sliced later), you have three options:

1) Forming them into small, approx. 1¼" (3 cm) 'walnut-sized' balls in the palm of your hand, then flattening in your palms, or putting them on the baking tray and then flattening them with a fork or your fingers until they are about ¼" (½ cm) thick; or,

2) Rolling the dough into 'logs' about 12" (30 cm) long, and the diameter you'd like your cookie to turn out, i.e. about 2" (5 cm). This log should be wrapped in clingfilm or greaseproof paper, labelled, and either refrigerated for a couple of hours before using, or frozen. When ready to use, slice the chilled cookie log into ¼" (½ cm) disks and arrange on the baking tray ready for cooking. This is a very convenient method, and I often use it for half a large batch of cookie dough, so that people can enjoy making a smaller amount with their hands in the first way, whilst having the convenience of the log to fall back on later. Even fairly wet doughs can be made into logs. The final alternative is:

FLAPJACKS

English flapjacks are similar to 'Muesli bars' in Australia or 'Granola bars' in the USA, but shouldn't be confused with thick American pancakes, which also go by the same name. Neither fully cake nor biscuit, these chewy bars, laden with oats and sweet golden syrup, stand in a class of their own. They were probably invented in Scotland, and are great for teas and hiking up mountains with. Turn to a flapjack whenever you need an energy boost! Rolled or regular porridge oats work best in this recipe.

For 6-8	For 50-60
5 oz (150 g/1¼ sticks) butter	2½ lb (1.1 kg)
3 oz (85 g/6 heaped tbsp) brown sugar	1½ lb (700 g)
3 oz (85 g/⅓ cup) golden syrup*	1½ lb (700 g)
8 oz (225 g/2⅔ cups) rolled oats	4½ lb (2 kg)
pinch salt	2 tsp
optional: 2 oz (55 g/⅓ cup) dried fruit/nuts	12 oz (350 g/2 cups)
(chopped apricots, cherries, dates, almonds, raisins, sunflower seeds etc.)	

1. Melt butter and syrup in a large saucepan. Do not boil. Keep the flame low and stir to avoid burning.

2. Add the sugar, oats, salt and any chopped nuts or fruit you may have chosen. Mix together.

3. Press into oiled tins approx. 1" (2 cm) thick. Smooth out top with back of a metal spoon.

4. Bake at 180°C (350°F, gas mark 4) for 30-40 minutes until set and golden brown. The flapjacks will stiffen a lot as they cool, so it's important to avoid overcooking them. If they become toffee-brown all over and very firm, they may look fine in the oven, but will be too hard once they've cooled.

5. When cool, cut into rectangular slices about 1" x 2½" (2½ x 6 cm).

    *If golden syrup is not available, try substituting thick honey. The resulting flapjacks will be a little less chewy and a little more crumbly, but still good.

HONEY AND LEMON COOKIES

Almost as delicious as the food at Schumacher College is the medicine. People who've caught colds, or brought them with them, will have fond memories of being made mugs of hot honey and lemon by our Director, Anne, and others. Everyone has their own way of brewing up this concoction, and it often includes ginger and cinnamon. It seems a shame, however, to reserve the delicious combination of honey and lemon just for those coldy and headachey moments of our lives. Why not make a cookie that follows the same theme—something to look forward to when you (or your patient) progress from sipping to crunching!

For 20-25 cookies	For 40-50 cookies
9 oz (255 g/2¼ sticks) butter	1 lb 2 oz (500 g)
3 oz (85 g/⅓ cup) honey	6 oz (170 g/⅔ cup)
1 lb (450 g/3 cups + 2 tbsp) white flour	2 lb (900 g)
3 oz (85 g/½ cup, heaped) caster/muscovado sugar	6 oz (170 g/1 cup)
1 pinch salt	½-1 tsp
1 tsp baking powder	2 tsp
juice of 1 medium organic lemon	juice of 2
zest of 2 organic lemons	zest of 4
1 egg yolk	1 egg
1 tbsp ground cinnamon	2 tbsp
½ tsp ground ginger (optional)	1 tsp (optional)

1. Put butter in mixing bowl and leave somewhere warm to soften for a few hours.

2. Add the flour, sugar, cinnamon, baking powder and salt to the butter. Break up the butter with a spoon or knife and then crumble it into the flour with your fingertips until a breadcrumb-like consistency is achieved.

3. Grate the lemons finely, removing just the outer yellow layer of the rind. This part, the zest, is lemony without being too bitter. Then add the egg, honey, lemon juice and lemon rind to the crumbly mixture. Mix well to form a soft dough.

4. Roll the dough into walnut-sized balls with your hands, i.e. roughly 1¼" (3 cm) round. Place on a parchment-covered baking tray 1½" (3-4 cm) apart from each other. Press balls down with the back of a spoon, a fork, or your fingers. They should be ¼-½" (½-1 cm) thick in the middle and there should still be at least a centimetre between each cookie, as they will spread a little.

5. Paint cookies with juice from the remaining zested lemons, sprinkle with sugar and cook in a medium oven for 15-25 minutes until they are beginning to turn brown at the edges. Cool for a few minutes before moving.

GINGER CRUMBLE SLICE

The recipe for this gingery, shortbready slice was inspired by three things: leftover crumble mix from a dessert, Grasmere gingerbread, and people asking for the recipe. It isn't always easy to re-create something you've concocted as a one-off simply to use up leftovers, but after several attempts, this recipe now comes close to the original re-hash.

Grasmere gingerbread, by the way, can only be bought in one shop in Grasmere, a small village in the Lake District. The recipe, which is a carefully guarded secret, has probably been made for centuries. Indeed, it must have been munched by the great nature poet William Wordsworth, who was an inhabitant of Grasmere.

20-25 slices approx.	40-50 slices approx.
9 oz (250 g/3 cups) rolled oats	1 lb 2 oz (500 g/6 cups)
12 oz (350 g/2½ cups) white flour	1 lb 9 oz (700 g/5 cups)
8 oz (225 g/1¼ cups) muscovado sugar	1 lb (450 g/2½ cups)
13 oz (365 g/3¼ sticks) butter	1 lb 10 oz (750 g/6½ sticks)
1 tbsp cinnamon or mixed spice	2 tbsp
2-3 tbsp ground ginger	4-6 tbsp
½ tsp salt	1 tsp
4 oz (110 g/¾ cup) crystallized ginger	8 oz (225 g/1½ cups)
4 fl oz (110 ml/½ cup) molasses	8 fl oz (200 ml/1 cup)

1. Put all ingredients except crystallized ginger and molasses together in a bowl. Rub the butter lightly into the dry ingredients until a crumbly mixture results. Avoid pressing it into one big lump. Add the finely sliced crystallized ginger and stir.

2. Stir in the molasses. You can use your fingers again once the molasses is partially integrated—otherwise they may get terribly sticky! However, there is no need to be too conscientious when combining the molasses with the rest, as part of the interest of this ginger slice is the way in which the molasses creates darker micro-hills in the areas where it falls. Therefore crumble it in only as much as necessary to obtain a dappled effect.

3. Now spread the mixture into an oiled tin, so that it is approx. ½" (1½ cm) thick at the most. Press it down slightly with the back of a metal spoon—just enough to allow the mixture to turn out a coherent whole and not a conglomeration of crumbs that will spill all over the floor when you bite it.

4. Cook in a moderate oven (180°C, 350°F, gas mark 4) for 30-40 minutes. When ready, ginger crumble slice should look dry on top, be quite firm and slightly browning. Cut into 1" x 2" (2 x 5 cm) fingers while still warm, and leave to cool before removing from tin, as the biscuit will need time to stiffen.

PEANUT CRUNCHETTES

Here is a crisp, nutty little cookie that can be made quickly and will be enjoyed by almost everyone.

For 45 cookies approx.	For 90 cookies approx.
9 oz (255 g/2¼ sticks) butter	1 lb 2 oz (500 g/4½ sticks)
8 oz (225 g/1⅓ cups) soft brown sugar	1 lb (450 g/2½ cups)
8 fl oz (225 ml/1 cup) golden syrup*	1 lb (450 g/2 cups)
1 lb (450 g/2 cups) crunchy peanut butter	2 lb (900 g/4 cups)
14 oz (400 g/3 cups) plain flour	1 lb 12 oz (800 g/5¾ cups)
4 oz (110 g/1 heaped cup) rolled oats	8 oz (225 g/2 heaped cups)
1 tsp bicarbonate of soda	2 tsp

1. Combine the butter, golden syrup, sifted brown sugar and peanut butter in a bowl. If necessary, leave in a warm place for the butter to soften for a while. Blend with a wooden spoon until a soft, creamy consistency is obtained.

2. Now combine the flour, bicarbonate of soda and oats with the mixture, to obtain a soft dough.

3. Roll the dough into small, walnut-sized balls and place 1" (3 cm) apart on a prepared baking tray. If the dough is too soft to roll with your hands, use a spoon to make walnut-sized dollops on the tray. Press down slightly with a fork—the cookies will spread a bit.

4. Cook in a moderate oven (180°C, 350°F, gas mark 4) until cookies are beginning to brown at the edges. Allow to cool on the baking tray for several minutes before attempting to move.

*If golden syrup is not available, substitute with honey, malt extract or molasses. These substances are stronger in flavour, but will still taste good. A reduced quantity of maple syrup could also be used.

SHORTBREAD

Traditional, tartan-wrapped Scottish shortbread is found for sale at all the airports and souvenir shops throughout the British Isles. It's called 'short' because the high butter content makes it mouthwateringly crisp and crumbly. An ideal gift that you can make at home: wrap it in silver foil and tie a tartan bow around it!

For 4-6	For 30
9 oz (255 g/2 scant cups) flour	1½ lb (675 g/5 cups)
6 oz (170 g/1½ sticks) butter	1 lb (450 g/4 sticks)
3 oz (85 g/6 heaped tbsp) caster sugar	8 oz (225 g/1 heaped cup)
pinch salt	½ tsp

1. Cut the butter into small pieces and lightly rub it into the flour and salt.

2. Add sugar and work the mixture by hand until it begins to hold together. Don't go on and on working the mixture until it becomes one shiny, textureless ball, as this can result in the shortbread becoming chewy rather than crumbly.

3. *Either* a) Shape into flattened rounds about 5-6" (12-15 cm) across and ½" (1 cm) thick. These may be fluted at the edges and scored with a knife to give 6-8 triangular pieces. Prick with a fork.

    Or b) Press into an oiled baking tray so that mixture measures about ½" (1 cm) thick and fills the whole tray. Prick all over with a fork.

4. Bake for 20-30 minutes at 170°C (325°F, gas mark 3) until golden brown. (It is possible to re-prick the shortbread when part-cooked or just ready, if you want the fork-prints to show.)

5. After allowing to cool slightly (but not entirely), slice into triangles or rectangular fingers (approx. 3" x 1"). If you accidentally allow the shortbread to cool too much and find it starts breaking when you try to cut it, then re-heat briefly in oven, and try again.

6. Optional: sprinkle with caster sugar before serving.

7. Variations: old recipes often substitute a little ground rice or semolina for a little of the flour, for texture: e.g. 1 oz (25 g/¼ cup) for the small quantity, 3 oz (85 g/¾ cup) for the large. Ground almonds can also be used in this way.

TWEET TWEET COOKIES

These biscuits would be a real hit on a bird table—they're laden with sunflower, pumpkin and sesame seeds. We usually make them vegan and wheat-free so that everyone can enjoy them. However they could equally be made with butter and brown flour if rye was not available. Their sweetness comes as much from malt extract and dates as from the relatively low proportion of muscovado sugar. As with many other vegan biscuits, the absence of eggs in the recipe makes them particularly vulnerable when first cooked, so they need to be left on the baking tray to cool and stiffen up before handling.

20-25 cookies	40-50 cookies
3 oz (85 g/3/4 cup) rye flour	6 oz (170 g/1 1/2 cups)
12 oz (340 g/4 cups) rolled oats	1 1/2 lb (700 g/8 cups)
9 oz (255 g/2 1/4 sticks) margarine	18 oz (500 g/4 1/2 sticks)
or 1/4 pint (150 ml/2/3 cup) sunflower oil	or 1/2 pint (280 ml/1 1/4 cups)
2-3 oz (55-85 g/6-8 tbsp) muscovado sugar	4-6 oz (110-170 g/3/4-1 cup)
1 cinnamon quill, ground	2 quills
3 oz (85 g/1/3 cup) tahini	6 oz (170 g/2/3 cup)
4 oz (110 g/2/3 cup) chopped dates	8 oz (225 g/1 1/2 cups)
2 oz (55 g/1/4 cup) malt extract	4 oz (110 g/1/2 cup)
2 oz (55 g/1/2 cup) sunflower seeds	4 oz (110 g/1 cup)
1 oz (25 g/1/4 cup) pumpkin seeds	2 oz (55 g/1/2 cup)
1 oz (25 g/1/4 cup) sesame seeds	2 oz (55 g/1/2 cup)
pinch of salt	1/2-1 tsp
optional: 1 egg yolk (if not vegan)	(1 egg)

1. If you want to make the arduous task of chopping dates a bit easier, soak them overnight in a little water. Then strain and chop. This is not necessary, but if you are cooking on your own with little time to spare, chopping all those leathery dates can become rather tedious.

2. Combine the rye flour, oats and sugar in a bowl. Lightly rub in the margarine, making a breadcrumb like mixture. Stir in the seeds, cinnamon, salt, and chopped dates. Now bind together with tahini and malt extract (and egg, if using). Mix thoroughly.

3. Press some of the mixture together in the palm of your hand, forming 2-3" (6 cm) flattened rounds. They can be about 1/4" (1/2-1 cm) thick in the middle, but not much more or they won't cook evenly. If your hands get too sticky, scrape the mixture off and flour them a little.

4. Place the cookies a little apart from each other on a prepared baking tray. Cook for 15-25 minutes in a moderate oven (180°C, 350°F, gas mark 4). When ready, they will be dry on top but feel slightly squidgy if pressed. When cool, they should be fairly crisp.

ALMOND SESAME BISCUITS

Sweet almonds, with their distinct yet delicate flavour, are considered by many people to be the Queen of nuts. They have been cultivated for centuries in warm Mediterranean countries such as Italy, and are now also grown in other warm climates such as southern California.

Grinding your own whole nuts in a food processor or nut mill will ensure that the ground almond is pure, and their skins will bring to the recipe a healthy amount of extra fibre. The appearance of the biscuits can be varied with different toppings: for example a solitary almond (whole or blanched), or a dense freckling of seeds. For almond-lovers, a few drops of pure almond essence may be added to the mixture to intensify the flavour.

30 biscuits	120 biscuits
7 oz (200 g/1½ cups) plain flour	1 lb 10 oz (750 g/5 cups)
2 oz (55 g/½ cup) almonds, ground	8 oz (225 g/2 cups)
3½ oz (100 g/½ cup, packed) muscovado sugar	14 oz (400 g/2 packed cups)
1 egg yolk	2 eggs
4½ oz (125 g/1 stick + 1 tbsp) butter	1 lb 2 oz (500 g/4½ sticks)
1 tsp cinnamon	2 tbsp
2 tbsp tahini	4 fl oz (110 ml/½ cup)
pinch of salt	1 tsp
1 tbsp sesame seeds	4 tbsp

milk to brush the biscuits; almonds, sesame seeds, and/or sunflower seeds for decoration

1. Measure all the dry ingredients into a bowl. (If you are grinding your own almonds, weigh them whole, then grind them.) Add the butter, break it up with a spoon, and then rub it in with your fingertips. Next add the egg and tahini and stir the mixture together with a wooden spoon until you can press it into a firm dough with your hands. Add more egg or a drop of oil if necessary.

2. The individual cookies can be formed in various ways, as described on page 158. Since this dough is quite firm and not too sticky or crumbly, it can also be rolled and shaped with biscuit cutters as follows. Lightly flour a flat, clean, surface. Roll out about a grapefruit-sized ball of dough at a time, using a floured rolling pin. Press the dough together at the edges with your fingers where it splits. Roll out thinly, about ¼" (½ cm) thick. Cut into rounds or other shapes using a cutter or an upturned glass. Line up biscuits on a prepared baking tray. Leave a little gap between each.

3. Brush sparingly with milk, then either press a whole almond into the centre of each biscuit, or take a little saucer of sesame seeds and press the biscuit into them, milk side down, to give a nice even, well-glued coating. Bake the biscuits at 180°C (350°F, gas mark 6) for 15-20 minutes until gently browning round the edges—though it's advisable to check them for even cooking after 10 minutes and move the tray around if necessary. Allow them to cool for several minutes before removing from the trays.

CLOCKWISE FROM TOP LEFT:
MARILYN'S VEGAN CHOCOLATE CAKE
WEDNESDAY FRUIT CAKE
DE LUXE DARK CHOCOLATE BROWNIES
GRANDMA HIRSH'S HONEY CAKE
MARILYN'S CHOCOLATE CAKE (SLICE)
COFFEE & WALNUT CAKE
CARROT CAKE (CENTRE)

1. Put butter and sugar in a bowl and leave in a low oven to soften for 5-10 minutes.

2. Prepare cake tins, oiling and lining.

3. Cream together butter, sugar and golden syrup.

4. Mix in the eggs.

5. Sieve together the cocoa powder, salt, flour and baking powder. Fold this into the mixture.

6. Dissolve bicarbonate of soda in the milk and stir this in. Mix well and pour mixture into the tins. If you are not going to ice the cake, sprinkle with sesame seeds/flaked almonds for decoration.

7. Cook in a moderate oven 180°C (350°F, gas mark 4) for 20-30 minutes until well risen, and firm but springy in the centre. (If you stick a knife or skewer in it will come out clean with no mixture sticking to it.) Allow to cool.

8. Cream together the filling ingredients, and sandwich the bases of the cakes together with the filling when completely cool.

9. Mix together the icing sugar and lemon until a thick creamy consistency is reached (not too runny, or it will all dribble off). Spread this over the top of the cake.

10. Alternatively, gently melt together the dark chocolate and butter in a double boiler. Add 1/4 tbsp liquid coffee if you like. Stir very gently, once the chocolate has gone soft—otherwise it can be temperamental and suddenly thicken. Spread over cake and leave to set.

"Eating with the fullest pleasure—pleasure, that is, that does not depend on ignorance—is perhaps the profoundest enactment of our connection with the world. In this pleasure we experience and celebrate our dependence and our gratitude, for we are living from mystery, from creatures we did not make and powers we cannot comprehend."

Wendell Berry

WEDNESDAY FRUIT CAKE

This is a light fruit cake suitable for feeding 50 hungry Totnesians at one of our weekly open evenings.

Small cake (10-12 slices)	Large cake (45-50 slices)
8 oz (225 g/1½ cups) plain flour	2 lb (900 g/5⅓ cups)
7 oz (200 g/1¾ sticks) butter	1 lb 9 oz (750 g/6¼ sticks)
7 oz (200 g/1 cup) demerara or granulated sugar	1 lb 9 oz (750 g/3½ cups)
2 tsp baking powder	3 tbsp
¼ tsp bicarbonate of soda + a little milk	1 tsp
pinch salt	½ tsp
2 tsp ground cinnamon	2 quills, ground (or 3 tbsp)
2 tsp mixed spice	2 tbsp
4 eggs	16
grated rind of 1 lemon and ½ orange	4 + 2
3 oz (85 g/½ cup) chopped dried apricots	12 oz (350 g/2 cups)
3 oz (85 g/½ cup) sultanas	12 oz (350 g/2 cups)
3 oz (85 g/½ cup) currants	12 oz (350 g/2 cups)
optional topping:	
½ oz (2 tbsp) chopped walnuts or sesame seeds	3 oz (85 g/¾ cup)

1. Cream together the butter and sugar. Gently beat in the eggs, two by two.

2. Mix together the flour, dried fruit, grated citrus rind, salt, baking powder and spices. Fold this into the other mixture.

3. Dissolve the bicarbonate in a little milk and add to the cake mixture. Add a little more milk if necessary, just enough to give a soft dropping consistency—not too runny.

4. Pour into a well greased/lined tin so the mixture is 1-1½" (2-3 cm) deep. (The large quantity will fill a 19"x11"/ 47 x 27 cm tin.) Sprinkle with chopped walnuts, sunflower or sesame seeds if desired.

5. Bake in a medium oven (180° C, 350°F, gas mark 4) for 30-45 minutes, until well risen and golden brown. The cake will be beginning to come away at the edges, and if you stick a knife or skewer in, it will come out clean and moist. Leave to cool, then cut into squares.

6. Variation: make a syrup with the juice of the lemons and 2 tbsp/8 tbsp sugar. Prick the top of the just-cooked cake all over. Spoon boiling syrup over.

RHUBARB AND GINGER CAKE

The long reddy-green stalks of the rhubarb plant are traditionally found growing in old chimney pots in an English cottage garden, where the hope is that they will turn out sweet, tender and pink. At Schumacher College, however, our gardener Peter Chambers lets rhubarb grow freely and abundantly, so that it takes over one corner of the herb garden with its enormous umbrella-like leaves. These leaves are said to be poisonous, and from the way visitors from abroad often react when they first see us preparing rhubarb, you'd think the stalks might be too. Not a bit of it—rhubarb is delicious in jams, fools and crumbles, particularly when accompanied with ginger and a fair amount of sugar.

In this recipe, rhubarb and crystallized ginger are chopped up and baked together in a cake. If you don't have access to rhubarb, try using peeled, chopped apples (which can be cookers) as a substitute.

For 10 approx.	For 50 approx.
4 oz (110 g/1 scant cup) wholewheat flour	1 lb (450 g/3 cups)
4 oz (110 g/1 scant cup) unbleached white flour	1 lb (450 g/3 cups)
½ tsp bicarbonate of soda	2 tsp
2 tsp ground ginger	3 tbsp
4 oz (110 g/1 stick) butter	1 lb (450 g/4 sticks)
4 oz (110 g/²⁄₃ cup) muscovado sugar	1 lb (450 g/2²⁄₃ cups)
2 fl oz (60 ml/¼ cup) black treacle/molasses	9 fl oz (250 ml/1 cup)
2 tbsp milk	4 fl oz (120 ml/½ cup)
2 eggs	8 eggs
2 oz (55 g/¹⁄₃ cup) crystallized ginger	8 oz (225 g/1¹⁄₃ cups)
12 oz (340 g/2 cups) chopped rhubarb or apples	2 lb 4 oz (1 kg/2 US quarts)

1. Remove leaves from rhubarb, plus any brown areas around the 'hoof' of the stem (although the white part is fine, and indeed relatively sweet). Rinse and dice into roughly ¾" (1 cm) pieces. Chop the crystallized ginger up quite finely. Mix together the flour, bicarbonate of soda and ginger powder. Add the chopped rhubarb and ginger to this and stir.

2. Melt the butter in a saucepan with the sugar and treacle (or molasses). Cool slightly. Blend the milk and egg into the cooled mixture, which can then be incorporated into the flour etc.. Mix well. Turn the mixture into prepared tin/s: these can be either loaf tins, or flatter tins. Both seem to work, but bear in mind that a deeper cake will take longer to cook. Make the mixture in a loaf tin not more than about 2" (5 cm) deep, to ensure even cooking.

3. Bake for 30-60 minutes at 180°C (350°F, gas mark 4) until cooked.

GRANDMA HIRSH'S HONEY CAKE

Debbie Hirsh first came to Schumacher College on the Ecological Economics course with Wolfgang Sachs in 1994. Later she returned to Schumacher College for a year as a helper, and shared her enormous culinary talents with us—and her collection of recipes. Here is a wonderfully simple and effective recipe for honey cake that Debbie's grandma used to make when her grandchildren came to tea. As it contains no butter, it's great for people avoiding lactose.

1 loaf	5-6 loaves
8 fl oz (250 ml/1 cup) clear honey	40 fl oz (1.1 litres/5 cups)
10 oz (280 g/2 cups) white flour	3 lb (1.3 kg)
2 tsp baking powder	3 tbsp
4 oz (110 g/½ cup) sugar	1¼ lb (600 g/2½ cups)
4 fl oz (110 ml/½ cup) water	1 pint (550 ml/2½ cups)
3 tbsp sunflower oil	7 fl oz (200 ml/1 scant cup)
2 eggs	9 eggs
pinch of ground ginger	1½ tsp
pinch of mixed spice	1½ tsp
handful of flaked almonds	5 oz (140 g/1 heaped cup) approx.

1. Beat together egg, sugar, oil, honey and about half the almonds.

2. Fold in flour, baking powder and spices. Stir in the water.

3. Pour mixture into prepared loaf tins, and sprinkle the tops with the remaining flaked almonds.

4. Bake for approximately one hour at 180°C (350°F, gas mark 4) until well-risen and golden brown.

5. Allow to cool in the tins (transfer on to a wire rack after 10 minutes if you're in a hurry.) Slice up when completely cool.

6. Variations: for a darker honey cake, substitute one third of the white flour with rye flour and use muscovado sugar. Sunflower seeds can also be used instead of flaked almonds.

SOPHISTICAKEY

This healthy cake, invented by Sophie Reynolds, is so sophisticated that it has a lot of that naughty-but-nice flavour you get when using butter, eggs, sugar and wheat, whilst in fact containing none of these. Sophie has been a vegan for many years, and observed a wheat-free diet during her time at the College. She firmly believes that vegan food can be just as delicious as any other, and shouldn't simply be imitative of dairy food. She experimented with this recipe until she arrived at something with the moistness and depth of texture she liked. We were surprised to find that hardened worshippers of dairy were soon poaching from the vegan box.

The recipe is written in fistfuls—that's as much as you can grab hold of in the palm of your hand and not drop. For those of us who suffer from shaky fingers, I can reveal that Sophie's fist grabs approximately 2 oz (55 g/^{2}/$_3$ cup) oats, flour or desiccated coconut, 4 oz (110 g/^{2}/$_3$ cup) raisins or cooked brown rice and 3 oz (85 g/^{3}/$_4$ cup) cashews.

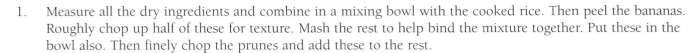

20 pieces approx.: 1 baking tin 12" x 10" (30 x 25 cm) approx.

2 fistfuls desiccated coconut
1 fistful raisins
1 fistful cashew pieces
3 fistfuls oats
2 fistfuls either brown rice flour, spelt flour or wholewheat flour
2 fistfuls cooked brown rice
4 tbsp sunflower oil
4-5 bananas
2-4 soaked prunes and 1-4 tbsp of their soaking water
1-4 tbsp apple juice concentrate

1. Measure all the dry ingredients and combine in a mixing bowl with the cooked rice. Then peel the bananas. Roughly chop up half of these for texture. Mash the rest to help bind the mixture together. Put these in the bowl also. Then finely chop the prunes and add these to the rest.

2. Now add the liquids: sunflower oil, prune juice and apple juice concentrate. Stir all the ingredients together, adding a little more prune juice or apple juice concentrate if necessary. (More apple juice will also make it sweeter.) The mixture should be moist and hold together like a wet dough or flapjack mixture.

3. Oil and line a baking tin with parchment. Press the mixture in and smooth it over with the back of a metal spoon. It should be approximately ^{3}/$_4$" (2 cm) deep.

4. Bake at 180°C (350°F, gas mark 4) for 30-40 minutes. The cake will be dry on top and quite springy. Leave to cool, then slice into squares. Store in an airtight container in the fridge.

MARILYN'S VEGAN CHOCOLATE CAKE

Marilyn Bruya came to Schumacher College in 1997 on James Hillman and Margot Maclean's course on 'Art, Consciousness and the Environment'. One day in the kitchen, we got on to the subject of how to celebrate vegan birthdays. Marilyn said she had a brilliant old Swiss recipe for chocolate cake that she always made for her daughter. Now her daughter has grown up and left home, but Marilyn still makes her the cake, freezes it and mails it through the post ready for her daughter's birthday. When it arrives, it's perfectly defrosted and ready to be topped with whipped cream and berries.

The whipped cream isn't vegan, of course, so try using vegan almond-honey cream instead, or just jam. Alternatively, sandwich the cakes together with raspberry or blackberry jam and whipped cream. Top with dark chocolate icing, or more cream. A liqueur can also be added. You'll be surprised how good a cake can taste without butter or eggs.

For 15 people	For 30 people
A: 11 oz (300 g/1½ cups) white sugar	1 lb 6 oz (650 g/3 cups)
15 oz (425 g/3 cups) white flour	1 lb 14 oz (850 g/6 cups)
2 oz (55 g/½ cup) cocoa	4 oz (110 g/1 cup)
2 tsp baking powder	4 tsp
1 tsp salt	2 tsp
B: 5 fl oz (150 ml/⅔ cup) light oil	10 fl oz (300 ml/1⅓ cups)
2 tbsp vinegar (preferably apple cider vinegar)	4 tbsp
2 cups (16 fl oz/470 ml) water	4 cups (32 fl oz/940 ml)
one or two 10" x 13" (25 x 32 cm) cake tins	two to four

1. Mix together all dry ingredients (A). Only use a spoon or egg whisk. Do not use an electric mixer. No substitutions! Then add all the wet ingredients (B) to (A). Marilyn says that any light vegetable oil will do (e.g. sunflower), but not olive oil. Pour cake mixture into ungreased cake tin(s). Bake at 180°C (350°F, gas mark 4) for 25-30 minutes.

2. When the cake is cool you may want to dress it up. Though Marilyn says it is good without frosting of any kind, she likes it topped with whipped cream and berries such as raspberries, or strawberries. For a vegan topping you could make the chocolate filling that goes with Julia's Chocolate Cake using margarine, or melt some plain chocolate, or press fresh berries into almond honey cream.

ALMOND HONEY CREAM (VEGAN)

How do you make a vegan birthday cake a little bit special when you can't use eggs, butter or cream? One way around the problem is to make this rich almond cream and sweeten it with a little honey. It can then be used to top or sandwich together vegan cakes, such as Marilyn's chocolate cake. It has almost the consistency of whipped cream (although it is richer), and can also be used to decoratively stick down fresh fruit. Often people with a lactose allergy will happily eat eggs, so you can, for example, make a carrot cake and top it with almond honey cream.

As in the vegan mayonnaise recipe, this recipe draws upon the emulsifying qualities of a protein, namely nuts, when whizzed together with oil.

Makes ½ pint (300 ml)

2 oz (55 g/½ cup) whole raw almonds
3 fl oz (85 ml/⅓ cup) soya milk
5 fl oz (140 ml/⅔ cup) sunflower oil
2-3 tsp lemon or orange juice
2-3 tbsp clear honey

Makes 3½ pints (2 litres)

12 oz (340 g/3 cups)
15 fl oz (400 ml/2 cups)
30 fl oz (850 ml/3¾ cups)
4-6 tbsp
5-8 fl oz (150-200 ml/½-1 cup)

1. Blanch the almonds by covering with boiling water. Leave for a minute, then slip off the skins.

2. Place the peeled almonds in liquidizer or blender of your food processor. Add half the soya milk. Blend until the almonds have totally merged with soya milk and lost any semblance of individual identity. Add remaining soya milk and blend again.

3. Remove insert in lid of blender and place on lowest setting. Drizzle in the oil in a thin stream until mixture thickens.

4. With blender still running, add lemon or orange juice. Blend for another few moments to allow mixture to thicken to desired consistency. (For a thinner pouring cream, add more soya milk.)

5. Blend in, or stir in, the runny honey. Sometimes the cream gets so thick that the liquidizer can no longer mix the ingredients properly. In this case, tip out the almond cream and mix in the honey, tasting for desired sweetness. Add any other seasonings you may wish to try—for example a little ground nutmeg, natural almond essence or finely grated orange rind.

6. Spread on cake, or store in fridge for up to a week in sealed container.

refrigerate fresh yeast, using the pure product will still be just as easy and cheaper. It is still what professional bakers prefer, which is why your local baker will have it to sell.

Easybake yeast may be useful as a standby, but I miss the presence of yeasty smells associated with the other two forms of yeast and not so much with this one. I also feel slightly suspicious of the process involved in creating such 'instant fix' products.

Warmth of water for activating yeast

When baking with yeast, your liquid (normally water, sometimes with milk added) should be blood heat: 90°-105°F (35°-38°C). It's the pleasant temperature you might like to find in a heated swimming pool, or use for bathing a baby.

Kneading yeast in dough

Absorbency of flours may vary from bag to bag, and therefore you will often find yourself adding a little more flour or water to your mixture. The perfect dough should be smooth to touch. If you poke it, nothing will stick to your finger, but you will feel that it is damp, springy, soft and highly elastic (more so if white flour has been used, as it contains a higher gluten content). It should be a pleasure to push, stretch and fold in the process of kneading. Protect your hands with a little flour. Normally, if the consistency is right, you will barely need to flour your working surface as the dough will not stick to it; you do not want to dry out the dough by adding more flour. If kneading dough by hand, 3 minutes is normally recommended to bring out the gluten and 'charm' the yeast. Normally if the first kneading is thorough, the second can be briefer, and more a matter of knocking-back as you smooth and shape the dough. Between kneadings, leave to rise in a warm place as described above.

Keeping yeast cosy

Almost as important as getting the right water temperature for the yeast, is finding the right warm and cosy spot for the dough to sit in whilst it proves. This may be a sunny window sill, a warm airing cupboard, or the (non-ignited) grill just above your pre-heated oven. The dough needs to sit for 40-60 minutes between kneadings until it has almost doubled in size. Spray the dough with water to stop a skin forming, or cover the bowl with a lid or cling film. Make sure the bowl is big enough to contain the doubled dough.

A final kneading

Once risen, punch the dough down and tip on to a lightly floured surface. Flour your hands and push the dough away from you. Then fold the outer edge to the inside. Turn slightly and push away from you again. The underside of the dough should become smooth and form the top of the loaf. The place where all the edges meet will become the bottom. When ready, shape it to fit your loaf tin—or bake round on a flat surface. Smooth with a sprinkling of flour.

Cutting corners

Having emphasized the importance of kneading, I would now like to contradict myself! The vitality of yeast is almost irrepressible, so if you really don't have much time for kneading, don't let that put you off. A thick, rather wet, well mixed, un-kneaded dough can simply be put in a tin, smoothed over with a wet hand, and left to rise. You can also miss out one rising, and just go for the single rising in the bread tin. The consistency may be slightly different, but the bread still very good. Similarly, though a warm spot is nice for dough when it suits you, sometimes you may want to put the dough in the fridge where it will rise slowly, ready for baking in the morning. Cut as many corners as you can, if time is stopping you from making your own bread—it is really so simple and such a pleasure. If you have a minimum of two hours at home, you should be able to fit it in with other things you are doing—just carry a timer with you to remind you that your bread is in process. It is the completion of breadmaking from start to finish that is time-consuming, not the personal attention you have to give it. Once it has become part of your routine, the psychological attention will not seem time-consuming either, and the results will be far more satisfying than a personal breadmaking machine could ever produce.

Testing and airing bread

Once the bread has been cooking for about an hour, it should be well-risen and golden brown on top. If you tip it out of its tin, the sides will also be light brown, and if you knock the bottom of the loaves there will be a satisfying hollow sound— a bit like knocking on a wooden door. Leave the loaf to cool on an airing tray. Leaving it in the tin can lead to a soggy bottom, as the steam cannot escape: instead it condenses and wets the outside of the bread.

FIGGY BREAD ROLL

A swirl of wholewheat bread encloses a medley of chopped fruit and nuts, which have been fused together with a coating of malt and honey. Once sliced, this figgy bread is delicious on its own, or buttered.

For 1 large loaf	For 3 large loaves
Dough	
1 lb (450 g/3 cups) wholewheat flour (or 85%)	3 lb (1.4 kg)
½ oz (10 g/1 tbsp) fresh yeast	1 oz (25 g/2 tbsp) fresh
or ¼ oz (5 g/1 heaped tsp) dried	or ½ oz (10 g/1 tbsp) dried
1 tbsp sugar	3 tbsp
1 tsp cinnamon or mixed spice	1 tbsp
2 tbsp sesame seeds	3 fl oz (100 ml/¾ cup)
10-11 fl oz (300 ml/1¼ cups) warm water	30-32 fl oz (900 ml)
½ tsp salt	1½ tsp
Fruit Filling	
6 oz (170 g/1 cup) dried figs, chopped	1 lb 2 oz (500 g/3 cups)
2 oz (55 g/⅓ cup) dried apricots, chopped	6 oz (170 g/1 cup)
2 oz (55 g/⅓ cup) dates, chopped	6 oz (170 g/1 cup)
2 oz (55 g/⅓ cup) raisins	6 oz (170 g/1 cup)
2 oz (55 g/½ cup) whole hazelnuts	6 oz (170 g/2½ cups)
(or chopped brazils)	
1 oz (25 g/¼ cup) sunflower seeds	3 oz (75 g/¾ cup)
2 oz (55 ml/¼ cup) clear honey	6 oz (170 g/¾ cup)
1 oz (25 g/2 tbsp) malt extract	3 oz (75 g/½ cup)
½ tsp cinnamon	1½ tsp
a little beaten egg (or soya dessert) to glaze	1

1. Combine all the dry ingredients for the dough, and rub in the fresh yeast, or add fast-acting yeast. (Mix traditional active dried baking yeast with warm water and sugar—see Yeast and Bread Baking).

2. Stir in the warm water, using enough of it to combine all the flour in a dough that's not too sticky. Cover loosely. Leave to rise in a warm place for 30-40 minutes.

3. Chop up all the dried fruit and rough chop the brazil nuts if you are using them.

4. Combine the dried fruit with the honey, malt extract, sunflower seeds, nuts and cinnamon.

5. When the dough has risen, knock it back, knead it a little and, on a floured surface, begin rolling it out into 1-3

large rectangles. Leave it to rest in between rollings, to obtain a good stretch. The dough should be about ½" (1 cm) thick.

6.   Sprinkle a few drops of water on the dough with your fingers, and then spread the fruit mixture over it, leaving about ½" (1 cm) of dough uncovered around 3 edges and slightly more along one length: about 1" (3 cm). The length represents the eventual length of the roll. Now roll up the dough, starting by carefully bending the wider edge of exposed dough over, and continuing to roll, and to press down on the roll, until you get to the other side. Keep the join underneath the loaf and give the loaf a firm pressing with your hands to make sure fruit and bread are all well glued together.

Press the ends together, using a little water to glue if necessary. Transfer on to a lined/oiled baking tray. Prick deeply all over with a fork or skewer, to allow air to escape. Paint with beaten egg and sprinkle with seeds and golden granulated sugar, if you wish.

7.   Leave to rise for 15-20 minutes and then bake at 180°C (350°F, gas mark 4) for 40-50 minutes. It should be lightly browned on top and sound hollow if tapped underneath.

FOCACCIA

Round, flat, or plaited, filled with onions, herbs, cheese, olives or sun-ripened tomatoes, all these are tantalizing, bountiful, variations on the theme of bread. All are representatives of a Mediterranean baker's culinary art that now bubbles vigorously in Britain, enlivening taste-buds tired from decades of square bread and white sliced sponge.

Focaccia is one of our favourite lunchtime breads at Schumacher College, and an excellent example of this baking phenomena. It's delicious served with cheese, or patés, or simply drizzled with olive oil and dunked in soup. In this recipe I've used strong white flour, but I often use a mix of 50% brown and 50% white.

For 8-10 (1-2 loaves) approx.	For 30-40 (4-6 loaves)
1-2 tbsp pine nuts (optional)	2 oz (55 g/$\frac{1}{2}$ cup)
1 oz (25 g) dried sun-ripened tomatoes	4 oz (110 g/1 heaped cup)
$\frac{1}{2}$ oz (10 g/1 tbsp) fresh yeast	2 oz (55 g/4 tbsp)
(or 1 heaped tsp dry yeast)	(or 4 tsp)
8-9 fl oz (250 ml/1 cup) warm water	1$\frac{3}{4}$ pints (1 litre/1 US quart)
1 lb (450 g/3 cups) unbleached white flour	4 lb (1.8 kg)
1$\frac{1}{2}$ tsp salt	1$\frac{1}{2}$ tbsp
1 tbsp oregano	4 tbsp
2 tsp muscovado sugar	3 tbsp
2 tbsp olive oil approx.	3 fl oz (100 ml/$\frac{1}{3}$ cup)
1 tbsp grated parmesan	1 oz (25 g/$\frac{1}{2}$ cup)
or cheddar cheese (optional)	

1. Soak sun-ripened tomatoes in boiling water for an hour or so, then chop roughly. Reserve the soaking water and include it in the bread (or soup).

2. Dissolve yeast in water and let froth, or crumble fresh yeast into flour. If using fast-acting dried yeast, sprinkle it straight into flour.

3. Mix liquid and yeast with flour, sugar, salt and tomatoes. Knead well. Leave for 30-40 minutes to rise.

4. Divide the dough into equal portions depending on how many loaves you want to make. Knead into smooth balls on a lightly floured work surface. Incorporate only as much flour as needed to stop the dough sticking to your hands. Sometimes no extra flour is necessary. Gently begin to flatten the dough-ball with your fist.

5. Using a rolling pin, roll into large flat rounds 1-1$\frac{1}{2}$" (2-3 cm) thick. Sometimes two rollings with a rest in between will overcome the elasticity of the dough and make it easier to roll flat.

6. Poke deeply with fingertips to make indentations.

7. Brush generously with olive oil, allowing it to run into the indentations and form small pools.

8. Sprinkle with dried oregano, and rock salt crystals.

9. Bake for 30-40 minutes at 180°C (350°F, gas mark 4). Sprinkle grated cheese on loaves after 20 minutes if you wish to use it—otherwise it will simply turn brown and dry. Serve while still warm, cutting into generous inch-thick (2 cm) slices or into wedges.

10. Variations: for olive and rosemary bread, substitute the sun-ripened tomatoes with double the quantity of pitted black olives (no need to chop). Add some chopped rosemary, and omit the pine nuts. For garlic fanatics, include whole peeled cloves of garlic in the tomato focaccia.

RYE SOUR DOUGH

Sourdoughs are great because they take advantage of the natural yeasts and sugar in the grain, but they take longer than yeasted bread to start proving. They can be boosted with use of a little yeast at the second stage. Once a 'starter' has been made from the first batch of dough, this can be used to encourage your second batch of dough to puff up much more quickly—perhaps within a few hours. Because the flour is left to soak for a longer time and has little or no yeast, the natural flavours of the grain are brought out to a far greater extent. The soaking also makes a bread that would otherwise be quite heavy, a little lighter.

1 loaf	3 loaves
1 lb 6 oz (600 g/4½ cups) rye flour	4 lb 2 oz (1.9 kg)
1 tbsp caraway seeds	3 tbsp
18 fl oz (500 ml/2¼ cups) warm water	52 fl oz (1.5 litres/1½ US quarts)
1 tbsp honey or brown sugar	3 tbsp
1 tbsp sunflower oil	3 tbsp
1 tbsp sesame seeds	3-4 tbsp
optional: ¼ tsp fresh or pinch dried yeast	½ tsp fresh or ¼ tsp dried

1. Mix together about two-thirds of the flour and all the water. A thick, yet sloppy mixture should be formed. Cover loosely with a tea towel and leave in a warmish place to prove.

2. Proving. The first proving is normally a matter of days rather than hours. However, be careful about leaving the sourdough too long in a very warm place, as the yeast activity may create alcohol (signalled by a vinegary smell). The dough, having risen, will flop and the bread will taste quite bitter. On average, leave the dough for about 2-3 days at room temperature—readiness will be signalled by the dough having puffed up slightly, and when you poke it, there will be little crackling sounds signalling activity, and perhaps some bubbles.

3. At this point, mix the rest of the flour into the dough. This will thicken the dough (which will have become runnier in the course of proving). Add the yeast dissolved in a little water to speed things up, if you like. Leave the (covered) dough for a few hours, or overnight.

4. Give a final stir. If you want to make another batch fairly soon, remove a few large spoonfuls of the mixture to act as a starter for the next dough so that the proving takes considerably less time. This starter mixture can be kept in the fridge in an airtight container until needed. Add salt, oil, honey and seeds to the rest of the dough and put into prepared tin/s. Leave to rise for 1-2 hours, then bake at 180°C (350°F, gas mark 4) for 1-1½ hours.

5. Using the starter. Combine the total quantity of flour with the water and starter. Leave to rise for several hours or overnight. Remove a few spoonfuls for your next starter, then add the other ingredients, and prove in prepared bread tins as before. Eventually your starter may lose its effect, and you will have to go back to the beginning again.

WHEAT- & GLUTEN-FREE CRISPBREAD

This crispbread recipe was given to me by a participant who was suffering from candida, and could not eat our normal bread as she was on a yeast- and gluten-free diet. It's a very simple recipe to prepare, once you've got hold of the flaky ingredients—which should be available in most health shops. Crispbreads are delicious whether you are on a special diet or not. Other flaked grains (oats, wheat, rye, etc.) can be used for variety by those who can eat them.

One batch

4 oz (110 g/1 cup) millet flakes
3 oz (85g/1 cup) maize flakes (or cornflakes)
4 oz (110 g/1 cup) rice flakes
4 oz (110 g/1 cup) buckwheat flakes
2½ oz (70 g/½ cup) linseed
3 oz (85 g/¾ cup) sesame seeds
1 oz (25 g/¼ cup) sunflower seeds
1 tbsp olive oil
1 tsp salt

1. Put all the above ingredients to soak with enough cold water to easily immerse everything when stirred.

2. After two hours or more, stir the mixture thoroughly. The consistency should now be like thick porridge. Pour away any superfluous liquid.

3. Take a flat baking tray and cover with baking parchment. Spread the mixture thinly and evenly over the parchment.

4. Bake at 160°C (310°F, gas mark 2½) for half an hour.

5. Slice into rectangles and bake for a further half hour.

6. If it is not quite dry, turn off the heat and leave the crispbread in the oven.

7. Variations: add spices such as caraway, and chopped herbs such as rosemary, coriander, basil and stinging nettles. For a slightly sweeter crispbread, add desiccated coconut and almonds.

CORNBREAD

Cornbread is a good accompaniment for bean stews. We find it works best when cooked in fairly deep tins, so the cooked cornbread is 2" (4-5 cm) deep, and light, spongy and golden when ready.

For 4-6	For 30
5 oz (140 g/1 cup) cornmeal (maize meal)	2 lb (900 g/6¼ cups)
3½ oz (100 g/¾ cup) unbleached white flour (or 50% brown & 50% white)	2¼ lb (1 kg/7 cups)
2-3 tsp baking powder	4 tbsp
½ tsp salt	2½ tsp
2 tbsp honey	6 fl oz (170 ml/¾ cup)
8 fl oz (250 ml/1 cup) milk	2½ pints (1.4 litres/1½ US quarts)
1 egg	6
2 tbsp melted butter or 2 tbsp sunflower/corn oil	6 oz (170 g/1½ sticks) or 6 fl oz (170 ml/¾ cup)

1. Melt the butter (or oil) and honey together. Whisk into the milk and eggs.

2. Sift the dry ingredients together. Add wet to dry ingredients and mix together quickly to make a batter.

3. Pour into a greased baking tin so that the mixture is at least 1" (2 cm) deep. Cook at 190°C (375°F, gas mark 5) for 30-40 minutes (small quantity) or 50-60 minutes (large quantity). When ready, cornbread will be golden brown and feel firm and springy. A knife will come out clean.

4. Slice into 2" (5 cm) squares. It's nice when served warm, but also good cold. Serve with butter, sour cream and beans.

5. *Special diets:* for people avoiding dairy, substitute milk with soya milk or rice milk and use oil not butter. However, don't attempt to leave out the eggs to make it suitable for vegans—you would be better off making a yeast-based cornbread, using half maize meal and half white flour. Spelt can be used instead of white flour for those who have an allergy to normal wheat flours.

DEVONSHIRE SCONES

Arriving in Queensland, Australia, Stephan and Julia were almost immediately met by signs advertising Devon Cream Teas. Rather disconcerting when you've just travelled for 24 hours in an aeroplane and think you've reached the other side of the world! It seems that the combination of scones, clotted cream and jam has migrated all over the world—along with the Brits.

For the original English tea shop experience, however, you need look no further than our beloved Totnes, which is riddled with delightful little teashops serving Earl Grey tea in silver tea pots and cake on lace doilies! To give a flavour of this tea-time heritage, we frequently treat participants coming to Schumacher College with a genuine Devon cream tea.

Scones are best described as halfway between bread and cake. They rise with baking powder and contain relatively little (or no) sugar. Clotted cream, meanwhile, is a thick buttery cream made by skimming the fatty skin off rich Jersey cow's milk that has been simmering on the stove. Use whipped double (or heavy) cream as a substitute if nothing similar is available.

Though scones are most delicious when still warm from the oven, they can also be prepared and eaten cold for convenience. Either way, slit them in half and generously heap clotted cream on each cut surface, then jam. (The Cornish, I'm told, prefer the jam first—which proves that it takes more than the globalization of a scone to stop you expressing regionality where it really counts!)

For 10 scones approx.	60 scones
8 oz (225 g/1²/₃ cups) white self-raising flour or 50%/ white & 50% brown flour	3 lb (1.4 kg)
(add 2 tsp baking powder if using plain flour)	(add 4 tbsp)
¼ tsp bicarbonate of soda (baking soda)	1½ tsp
2 oz (55 g/½ stick) butter, softened	12 oz (350 g/3 sticks)
1 egg, beaten	6
6 tbsp milk approx.	1 pint (550 ml/2½ cups) approx.
1 tsp ground cinnamon or mixed spice	2 tbsp
pinch salt	1-2 tsp
1½ tbsp sugar	4 oz sugar (110 g/½ cup) approx.
2 oz (55 g/⅓ cup) sultanas or raisins (optional)	12 oz (350 g/2 cups)
4 oz (110 g/½ cup) clotted cream, approx.	1½ lb (700 g) approx.
4 oz (110 g/½ cup) strawberry or other jam	1½ lb (700 g) approx.

1. Combine the flour, sugar, bicarbonate of soda (baking powder), cinnamon (or mixed spice) and salt in a mixing bowl.

2. Cut the butter into this. Leave it to soften in a warm place if necessary, then rub the butter into the flour lightly and quickly with your fingertips, until a crumbly consistency is achieved.

3. Make a well in the middle of the mixture, and add the beaten eggs and most of the milk. Mix ingredients together until a very soft (but not sticky) dough is formed. Add a little more milk if the mixture seems too dry.

4. Tip the dough on to a floured table top. Take a quarter of the dough at a time if you have made the larger quantity. Roll it out lightly with a floured rolling pin until about 3/4" (2 cm) thick.

5. Take a 1 1/2-2" (4 cm) round metal pastry cutter and press it sharply into the dough. If you have no cutter, use the open end of a small glass or jar, dipped in flour, or cut into triangles with a knife. Knead together all the dough you have not used first time round. Roll it out again and cut some more scones, until it is all used up.

6. Place scones on a prepared baking tray. Brush with any remaining milk or dust with flour.

7. Bake for about 15 minutes at 190°C (375°, gas mark 5) until well risen and golden brown.

8. Heap the scones on to a serving plate. Accompany with a bowl of clotted cream and a bowl of jam (typically strawberry). Let the friendly aromas announce to your family or guests that tea is ready!

CAPTAIN W's ENDPAGES

William Thomas, the College's House Manager, is a man of very particular knowledge: how to close doors without squeaks, how to make videos, how to make wind chimes, how to make breakfast last all day, how to turn sunbathing into an official duty. He is also the person who knows best how to keep the place clean and tidy, and how to involve everyone in the process without anyone really thinking that it's work. Well, perhaps it isn't.

William arrived at Schumacher College in January 1992, on the eve of its first birthday. He had come to spend a weekend with his sister Karen, who taught movement and coordinated creative 'happenings' at the College. He was on his way between Spain and Yorkshire—and he never left. Almost ten years later, it's difficult to imagine the college without William: without his electronic diary beeping in the middle of staff meetings, without his curious adventures, ingenious solutions and frequent disappearances to Spain, to Yorkshire—and into all sorts of cupboards no one else knows about. The most often repeated phrase at the College is, it seems, "Where's William?"

One little known aspect of William's expertise is his culinary knowledge. Here he reveals all . . .

How to Boil an Egg

There are three details to remember: 1. Use a drawing pin (thumbtack) to make a hole in the big end. 2. Start with boiling water, not cold. 3. Use only ⅜" (1 cm) of water, but put the lid on the pan. You steam the egg.

Times: Small egg 4:30 minutes   Medium egg 4:45 minutes

Large egg 5:00 minutes   Hard boil 6:00 minutes

An egg has an air sac in the big end. Making the pinhole allows the egg's flesh to expand into this space, forcing the air out. You'll see the little bubbles appear. This way, the shell doesn't crack. Steaming the egg with the lid on is just as efficient as boiling it underwater as long as the ½" (1 cm) of water is boiling rapidly. It also saves a lot of energy. Use a watch or clock with a second hand: the timings need to be fairly precise, and will produce an egg whose white is hard and whose yolk is soft and tacky. But beware if you live at altitude: water boils at a lower temperature there and you will have to allow a longer cooking time.

Sprouted green lentils or mung beans

Sprouted lentils are highly nutritious and delicious in a salad, in a stir-fry, or on their own with dressing. Here's how to prepare them.

1. Soak underwater (without lid is OK) overnight.

2. Rinse and drain twice. Cover loosely with lid in (e.g.) a plastic box.

3. Put somewhere reasonably warm and shady.

4. Each day, and preferably twice a day, rinse, drain and loosely cover.

5. When the roots are ¹/₂" (1 cm) long and the shoots start to form, give a final rinse and put beansprouts in the fridge (or use). Once sprouted, they will become 4-5 times greater in volume.

The Concept

First you have to reawaken the lentil: turn it from a dry object back into a hydrated object like it was when it was born. But when it comes alive, it's a living thing and needs oxygen, so don't drown it. From then on, like all living things it has a metabolism which produces waste products which you have to rinse away or they will poison the lentil. And all the time it needs a damp, reasonably dark environment just like it would experience in moist soil; a loose lid keeps moisture in, but doesn't suffocate. The roots are soft but the shoots are fibrous, so you don't want the leafy shoots to grow. Putting the sprouts in the fridge reduces metabolism (and therefore growth) to very low levels without killing the plants, and as long as you rinse them once in a while, they will keep for several days.

(P.S. you can't use red split lentils. They have been split and are as dead as a doornail.)

Deep Fried Seaweed

Serve as a salty, thirst-inducing crudité before a meal. It's full of iron and minerals.

Method

Use kombu or wakame. Cut the strands across the grain with scissors into ¹/₂" (1 cm) lengths. Heat an inch (2.5 cm) of sunflower oil in a wok or small deep pan until smoking hot, then toss in the seaweed and roll it around for no more than 1 minute and possibly as little as 15 seconds. Remove with a large perforated spoon as soon as the seaweed has stopped spitting and unfolding.

Soaking Nuts

Soaking any kind of nut or seed overnight improves it. Why? Because it has been brought to life! It thinks will soon become a plant, and starts producing the sugars and complex proteins necessary for growth. Peanuts (groundnuts) in particular are transformed by soaking. They become crunchy and much tastier, a bit like water chestnuts. Experiment, too, with sunflower seeds and almonds. Try adding soaked nuts to salads.

William's Masala Chai

No sooner have we finished eating supper on a Wednesday evening, than William disappears into the kitchen and starts to grind spices. He's continuing the tradition of making hot spicy chai (tea) to serve after open evenings. This was first introduced to Schumacher College by Bruce Easton Kings, a very lyrical green man who left the college to walk, juggle and teach his way through India and Japan in the name of peace. During the Indian leg of the peace walk, Bruce and the other walkers were accompanied by cyclists who pedalled alongside with kettles of warm chai to keep everyone sweet. Masala chai can also be served up after an Indian meal, such as the delicious bhojan concocted by the College's other great peace-walker, Satish.

Sometimes I wonder if it is the aroma of cardamom and that lures so many people to make their own pilgrimage to the College every open evening—but perhaps that is irreverent. Of course, it's our brilliant teachers! The chai just prevents them being asked too many awkward questions at the end of their talks. Try following William's instructions and see what you think. And now, over to him:

The main thing about chai is that it's boiled up in a pan with lots of milk (25%-50%) and sugar. In North India they don't always add spices, but in the Western world we should add spices just to remind us what it is we're drinking. The most important spice in chai is cardamom (ground up or crushed) and after that you can take your pick from cinnamon, cloves, ginger and black pepper. Choose an ordinary kind of black tea bag: Earl Grey is far too fancy. At Schumacher College, when I make chai for the open evening guests, I make one pan of soya milk chai too. This is really a slight travesty of the chai concept, but necessary when there are vegans about.

For 4-5	For 50
2 thin slices ginger root (or ¼ tsp ginger powder)	2 (or 3 tsp)
2 cardamom pods, crushed	20
1 clove	20
1 cm (½") of cinnamon quill or ½ tsp powder	2 quills or 2 tbsp
3 cups boiling water	12 pints (7 litres/7½ US quarts)
2 cups full fat (whole) milk (or soya milk)	8 pints (4.5 litres/4¾ US quarts)
2 tea bags (use the ordinariest)	20 tea bags
4 tsp sugar (to taste)	8 oz (225g/1 heaped cup) approx.

Method

To make chai, crush or grind cardamom pods, cloves, and broken cinnamon flute in a spice grinder. Put three cups of boiling water in a pan with one or two cups of full cream milk. Throw in tea bags, sugar, and the spices. When the chai has reboiled, causing the milk to produce froth, fish out the tea bags with a small sieve and let the spices steep for at least 2 minutes (preferably half an hour). Reheat the chai if necessary and strain. Chai-wallahs in India pour the chai rapidly back and forth between two pans to improve texture. Always serve chai in glasses or small clay tumblers, never in cups.

BOOKLIST

Vegetarian Cooking

The Art of Indian Vegetarian Cooking, Yamuna Devi and Bala Devi, Bala Books.

The Bean Book, Rose Elliot, Fontana Original.

The Chocolate Book, Helge Rubinstein, Penguin Books.

The Cranks Recipe Book, David Canter, Kay Canter and Daphne Swann, Grafton Books.

Delia Smith's Book of Cakes, Delia Smith, Coronet Books.

Eastern Vegetarian Cooking, Madhur Jaffrey, Jonathon Cape.

Eat Your Greens, Sophie Grigson, Network Books.

The Enchanted Broccoli Forest, Mollie Katzen, Ten Speed Press.

The Greens Cookbook, Deborah Maderson and Ed Brown, Bantam Doubleday Dell Publishing Group.

Madhur Jaffrey's World Vegetarian Ebury Press.

Middle Eastern Vegetarian Cookery, David Scott, Rider Books.

The New Moosewood Cookbook, Mollie Katzen, Ten Speed Press.

Sundays at Moosewood Restaurant, by the Moosewood Collective, Fireside Books.

The Supreme Vegetarian Cookbook, Rose Elliot, Fontana/Collins.

Tassajara Cooking and *Tassajara Recipes,* Edward Espe Brown, Shambhala Publications / Zen Centre.

The Tassajara Bread Book, Edward Espe Brown, Shambhala Publications.

Tomato Blessings and Radish Teachings, Edward Espe Brown, Riverhead Books.

Vegetarian Cooking for Everyone, Deborah Maderson, Broadway Books.

The Vegetarian Epicure, Anna Thomas, Vintage Books.

General Cookery

Delia Smith's Complete Cookery Course, and *How to Cook* (2 vols) BBC Publications.

Good Housekeeping Cookery Book, Ebury Press.

Joy of Cooking, Irma S. Rombauer and Marion Rombauer Becker, J.M. Dent & Sons, London.

Health, Nutrition & Special Diets

Catering for Health and Special Diets, Maurice Newbound, G.S. Publications.

The Complete New Herbal, Richard Mabey, Penguin Books.

Complete Nutrition, Dr Michael Sharon, Prion Books.

Healing with WholeFoods— Oriental Tradition and Modern Medicine, Paul Pitchford, North Atlantic Books.

Healing Foods, Dr Rosy Daniel, Thorsons.

Healing Foods Cookbook, Jane Sen, Thorsons.

The Organic Baby and Toddler Cookbook, Daphne Lambert & Tanyia Maxted-Frost, Green Books.

The Vegan Cook Book, Nicola Graimes, Lorenz Books.

The Vegan Cookbook, Alan Wakeman and Gordon Baskerville, Faber & Faber.

Food Politics & Local Economics

Diet for a Small Planet, Frances Moore Lappé, Ballantine Books. New York.

Farms of Tomorrow Revisited (Community Supported Agriculture), Trauger Groh & Steven McFadden, distributed by Chelsea Green (USA) and Green Books (UK).

Food First, Frances Moore Lappé and Joseph Collins, Abacus. (An action plan to break the famine trap.)

Genetic Engineering and You, Moyra Bremner, HarperCollins.

Genetic Engineering, Food, and our Environment: A Brief Guide, Luke Anderson, Green Books (UK), Chelsea Green (USA).

Going Local-Creating Self-Reliant communities in a Global Age, Michael Shuman, Free Press.

Local Harvest, Kate de Selincourt, Lawrence and Wishart.

The Organic Directory, Clive Litchfield, Green Books/Soil Association.

Our Stolen Future, Colburn, Dumaroski & Peterson Meyters, Abacus. (About the effects of plastics on the environment and health.)

Short Circuit: Strengthening local Economics for Security in an Unstable World, Richard Douthwaite, Green Books (UK), New Society (USA).

World Hunger: 12 myths, Frances Moore Lappé, Joseph Collins and Peter Rossett, Grove Press (USA).

Ecological Inspiration

Small is Beautiful, E. F Schumacher, Abacus.

Guide for the Perplexed, E.F. Schumacher, Abacus.

The Turning Point, Fritjof Capra.

Ancient Futures, Helena Norberg-Hodge, Sierra Club Books.

Gaia: The Practical Science of Planetary Medicine, James Lovelock, Gaia Books.

No Destination: An Autobiography, Satish Kumar, Green Books (UK). US edition: *Path without Destination* by William Morrow.

NETWORK ADDRESS LIST

Schumacher College
The Old Postern
Dartington Hall
Devon TQ9 6EA
Tel 01803 865934
Fax: 01803 866899
schumcoll@gn.apc.org
www.gn.apc.org/schumachercollege/
(including 'The Lost Recipes of
Gaia's Kitchen'!)

**Biodynamic Agricultural
Association**
Painswick Inn Project
Gloucester Street
Stroud, Glos. GL5 1QF
Tel: 01453 759 501 (9am-1pm)

**Campaign for Food
Safety/Organic Consumers Action**
860 Highway 61, Little Marais,
Minnesota 55614, USA
Tel. 218-726-1443
Fax. 218-226-4157
oca@purefood.org
www.purefood.org

Centre for Alternative Technology
Machynlleth, Powys
Wales SY20 9AZ
Tel: 01654 702400
info@cat.org.uk www.cat.org.uk

Corporate Watch
16b Cherwell Street
Oxford OX4 1BG
Tel: 01865 791 391
Fax: 01865 243 562
mail@corporatewatch.org
www.corporatewatch.org

Elm Farm Research Centre
Hamstead Marshall, Nr Newbury
Berks RG20 0HR
Tel: 01488 658298
Fax: 01488 658503
elmfarm@efrc.com
www.efrc.com

**Ethical Consumer Research
Association**
Unit 21, 41 Old Birley Street
Manchester M15 5RF
Tel: 0161 226 2929
Fax:0161 226 6277
ethicon@mcr1.poptel.org.uk
www.ethicalconsumer.org

The Fairtrade Foundation
Suite 204, 16 Baldwin's Gardens
London EC1N 7RJ
Tel: 020 7405 5942
Fax: 020 7405 5943
mail@fairtrade.org.uk
www.fairtrade.org.uk

Five Year Freeze Campaign
94 White Lion Street
London N1 9PF
Tel: 020 7837 0642
Fax: 020 7837 1141
gealliance@dial.pipex.com
www.dspace.dial.pipex.com/gealliance

The Food Commission
94 White Lion Street
London N1 9PF
Tel : 020 7837 2250
Fax : 020 7837 1141
foodcomm@compuserve.com
www.foodcom.org.uk

The Genetics Forum
94 White Lion Street
London N1 9PF
Tel : 020 7837 9229
geneticsforum@gn.apc.org
www.geneticsforum.org.uk

**Henry Doubleday Research
Association**
Ryton Organic Gardens
Ryton-on-Dunsmore, Coventry,
West Midlands CV8 3LG
Tel: 01203 303517
Fax: 01203 639229
enquiry@hdra.org.uk
www.hdra.org.uk

The Pesticides Trust
Eurolink Centre, 49 Effra Road
London SW2 1BZ
Tel: 020 7274 8895
Fax: 020 7274 9084
pesttrust@gn.apc.org
www.gn.apc.org/pesticidestrust/
Coordinator: David Buffin

**ITDG (Intermediate Technology
and Development Group)**
ITDG Publications
103-105 Southampton Row
London WC1B 4HH
Tel: 0207 436 9761
orders@itpubs.org.uk
www.itpubs.org.uk

**Institute for Food and
Development Policy (Food First)**
398 60th Street
Oakland, CA 94618-1212
Tel: (510) 654 4400
foodfirst@igc.apc.org
www.foodfirst.org

**International Society for Ecology
and Culture (ISEC)**
UK: Foxhole, Dartington
Devon TQ9 6EB
Tel: 01803 868650
Fax: 01803 868651
isecuk@gn.apc.org
www.isec.org.uk
USA: PO Box 9475,
Berkeley, CA 94709
Tel: 510 548 4915
Fax: 510 548 4916

**National Association of Farmers'
Markets**
South Vaults, Green Park Station
Green Park Road
Bath BA1 1JB
Tel: 01225 787914
Fax: 01225 460840
nafm@farmersmarkets.net
www.farmersmarkets.net

Organic Farmers and Growers
50 High Street, Soham
Ely, Cambridgeshire CB7 5HF
Tel: 01353 722 398
Organic Food Federation
Tithe House, Peaseland Green
Elsing, East Dereham
Norfolk NR20 3DY
Tel: 01362 637 314

The Schumacher Society
The CREATE Environment Centre
Smeaton Road
Bristol BS1 6XN
tel/fax: 0117 903 1081
schumacher@gn.apc.org
www.oneworld.org/schumachersoc

Seeds of Change
P.O. Box 15700
Santa Fe, NM 87 506, USA
Tel: 505-438 7052
gardener@seedsofchange.com
www.seedsofchange.com

The Soil Association
Bristol House, 40-56 Victoria St.
Bristol BS1 6BY
Tel: 0117 9290661
Fax: 0117 925 2504
info@soilassociation.org
www.soilassociation.org

Sustain
94 White Lion Street
London N19PA
Tel: 0207 8371228
Fax: 0207 8371141
sustain@sustainweb.org
www.sustainweb.org

**WWOOF (Willing Workers on
Organic Farms)**
Each country has its own office.
For information, visit the WWOOF
website : www.wwoof.org
contact for WWOOF UK:
Fran Whittle
PO Box 2675, Lewes
East Sussex BN17 1RB

INDEX